END

(Earth's Nuclear Deterrent)

PRITCHARD-JONES
E N D (Earth's Nuclear Deterrent)
65
9781

SPECIALISATION.

CENTRAL RESERVE STOCK

END

(Earth's Nuclear Deterrent)

HUGH PRITCHARD-JONES

CHRISTOPHER DAVIES (Publishers) LTD.

LLANDYBÏE   CARMARTHENSHIRE

This book is respectfully dedicated

to

WOMEN

CONTENTS

Y GWIR YN ERBYN Y BYD

(Truth Against the World)

FOREWORD

When Mr. Pritchard-Jones called to see me and asked me if I would write a Foreword for his new book, Earth's Nuclear Deterrent, I told him I was sure that I was not the person to write anything of the kind. He explained that his book was concerned with the urgent need of understanding and tolerance between nations, if they were not going to destroy themselves, and he said he felt that I was one of those who had done something to further through music a possible unity between peoples. I tried to say that I was really concerned with musical harmony among men.

I have for years been interested in the national musical expression of my country, and this has led me to be deeply interested in the national musical expressions of other countries. In this way I have come to realize the fundamental differences that exist between the folk-music expressions of different peoples. This has forced me to wonder at the existence of an internationally accepted supranational musical notation and idiom. This appears to me to be the most wonderful achievement of international human effort and agreement. Practically all the different nations of Europe, America, Australia and parts of Asia and Africa are using the same simple eight-note musical scale for international music-making, and at the same time retaining ancient traditional inflected scales that have for centuries expressed their deepest national emotions. The internationally accepted music of the great composers of America, Austria, Bohemia, Britain, Czechoslovakia, France, Germany, Hungary, Italy, Norway, Russia, Spain, etc., is all written using this note relationship of the sounds of the first syllables of the first six lines of the sixth century Hymn to St. John, which simple scale with a leading note added was devised by a Benedictine Monk in the eleventh century so that all the people of the Christian Church could sing together one song to God!

Perhaps the simple sounds of a hymn may be the means yet of saving man from himself. Anyway, it may be that the readers of Mr. Pritchard-Jones's book will hope so.

W. S. GWYNN WILLIAMS.

Llangollen, 1965.

INTRODUCTION

'Poor England! Leading her free, careless life from day to day, amid endless good-tempered Parliamentary babble, she followed, wondering, along the downward path which led to all she wanted to avoid.'

'If only the British people could have known and realised . . . history might have taken a different turn.'

Churchill: *The Gathering Storm.*

ENDLESS good-tempered Parliamentary babble! Evocative of the euphonic word-picture, ' In every babbling brook, he finds a friend.' The Parliamentary babble of those days of bungled opportunities, however, was no friend of Churchill, as the Churchill of the 'thirties knew only too well.

The Gathering Storm was written in the second half of the 'forties, well after the Second World War had rocketed Churchill to the pinnacle of power and fame.

In the infinitely more momentous 'sixties, the British people are again slithering down the path that leads to all they want to avoid, and, because, this time, not a turn, but the end of history is the penalty of ignorance, the urgent need is truth and nothing but the truth.

What is the Party Political System supplying? Bitter vituperation, even in the decorous House of Lords. On Wednesday, the 5th November, 1964, Lord Dundee spoke of ' The really outrageously fictitious and unfair accusation by the Prime Minister, repeated by Mr. Brown, that the late government, and particularly Mr. Maudling, had deliberately concealed the facts of the economic situation for electoral reasons . . . it is the Prime Minister who is deliberately exaggerating the balance of payments position in order that he, later on, may be able to pose as the man who had delivered the Country from an economic crisis which has never existed. I can only record now . . . my opinion that it is probably the Prime Minister and not Mr. Maudling who is seeking to deceive the country.' (Loud Opposition cheers.)

The reason for the concerted run upon the Pound was discussed on Thursday, the 26th November, 1964, in the television programme, 'Gallery', of the BBC.

With scrupulous fairness, Mr. McKenzie and Mr. Trethowen let films provide proof of what the Leaders of the two major Political Parties had said of the economic condition of Britain up to the time of the General Election of October 1964. Their impartiality and sense of responsibility, together with the judicial summing up of the economist, Mr. Shanks, contrasted sharply with the special pleading of the two Members of Parliament who also took part. The concern of the latter was Party, the concern of the former, the truth. A Parliamentary State indeed: what we have in Britain to-day is a Party State.

In practice, as I point out, in the Soviet Union: Another Look, each of the two major Political Parties relies upon a solid block-vote of mindless partiality. To win a General Parliamentary Election, a Leader has to retain or detach a certain percentage of the 'floating voters'. To do so, each Leader dresses up as a Father Christmas and denounces the other as a dangerous imposter. Often enough, a swing-over of 5% is enough to make a Leader of Party the Prime Minister of Britain, who, according to recent practice, can assert his will unchallenged, even to dismissing half of the Cabinet at a moment's notice as a diversionary tactic.

This is the effect of Party to-day, whatever the consequence to the Country. In the financial crisis of November 1964, the sedation of Europe became vital for Britain. Did the warring Party Leaders stop to think that between them they represented practically the whole electorate, the whole adult population of Britain? Reckless Party warfare so besmirched our reputation, so frightened Europe that the run on the Pound became a stampede.

For years, 'The British Sickness' has been a talking point in Europe! Even among those who are not habitual Anglophobes. In an increasingly competitive world, this reputation is fraught with grave peril to Britain, a peril recklessly disregarded in the obsessional Party warfare of November

10

1964. What a political system! What a relief to read Graham Hutton's article: Cutting the Old Party Cackle! In it he writes: ' One New Year resolution we should all make is to overhaul our political ideas . . . in our sixth economic crisis since the war ended nearly 20 years ago (we should) be wondering whether our party-political, governmental system —or lack of it—may be at fault.' And what a Europe! In 1940 she was dust beneath the Nazi heel, her resuscitation dependent upon Britain. Unless the same moral might intervene in time, Europe will again be dust, this time radio-active.

In so far as the easier relations between France and Germany brought about by Adenauer and De Gaulle, in so far as the groupings of the Countries of the West represent a new balance of power in a divided world, in what way does the fatal symbol of the old division differ from the new? The old symbolised conventional war: the new, thermo-nuclear. The old symbolised the graves of millions: the new symbolises the grave of Man.

With her unique experience of standing alone, I believe Britain has it in her to make goodwill and truth prevail.

To achieve fulfilment, however, Britain must unite, and, for a time at any rate, put behind Party Warfare with its brawling accusations, counter-accusations and degrading imputations: behaviour unthinkable in private life, be-haviour unworthy in any life.

I believe Britain would be galvanised into action by news of an agreement between Party Leaders to serve in a National Government dedicated to survival under the over-all leadership of the Prime Minister of the day. If we are to survive we must rise out of the Party rut, down which we are again slithering to all we want to avoid. Incidentally, is not the plea for non-party policies on immigration and defence an admission of inadequacy, weakness and danger in Party warfare? And is not the same thing proved by the report in March 1965 of the Milner Holland Committee appointed by a Conservative Government in August 1963 to investigate racketeering and slums? According to the report,

11

housing has been the 'sport' of political prejudice, and the Chairman has described housing as political dynamite. Consider, too, the appointment of a former Conservative Minister to the Chairmanship of the Prices and Incomes Board on the nomination of a Labour Minister. Some Conservatives, forgetful of the New Party Image of Du Cann, expressed relief at the departure of the 'miner's' son. If any Minister must succeed, that Minister is George Brown. If any Minister is one hundred per cent. eager to succeed for the sake of Britain, that Minister is George Brown. It may certainly be taken for granted, therefore, that Mr. George Brown nominated Mr. Aubrey Jones because he believed Mr. Aubrey Jones is the man most likely to achieve success. Now, an incomes policy is indispensable not only for prosperity and full employment in Britain, but also for the well-being of a world that needs for its survival a strong independent Britain. Through no fault of their own, however, certain Trade Unionists, like certain Conservatives, cannot think in national terms. Fortunately for them and for us all, Mr. George Brown and Mr. Aubrey Jones can. Indeed, as the grave problems of housing, immigration, defence and independence are bedevilled by Party Politics, so is our existence.[1]

---

[1] The *Daily Telegraph*, 25th of January, 1965, writing of Churchill after the General Election of 1945:
'As Leader of the Opposition he had worked arduously, and with a moving sincerity, for European co-operation.
' His speeches to the International Council of the European Movement and at the Congress of Europe and the Council of Europe bore eloquent testimony to his passionate desire for unity among the Western Nations.'
Hence, on his return to power as Prime Minister, the movement for European unity was expected to surge forward; but, as Churchill himself said: 'The Party Machine was too strong for me.'
Corroboration may be found on page 13 of the Obituary Supplement of the *Daily Telegraph*, again of the 25th of January, 1965:
' It is true that there was always an undercurrent of grumbles against him as a party leader. His powers of debate and repartee were quenchless, but his genius did not run to the sour attritional tactics of party warfare.'
' Peace,' said Churchill in 1951, ' is the last prize I have left to win.' This was also true of President Eisenhower. The Party System, the Usurpers and the Establishment defeated them.

But Party Politics are not the only rut. Consider the idealists outside Party Politics. CND, for instance. From the beginning, almost, it split into two groups, the Russell and the Collins. The Russell group split again, and, in turn, Collins resigned from the one associated with his name. As they divide, so do they lose virtue and dissipate all prospect of achievement. Unity is strength: division is destruction. United as constitutional campaigners for a national government committed to survival, they could help to make the whole electorate an instrument to save the world from the calamitous war that, this time, will definitively end war.

It was 'rubric obsessionalism' in Germany that prevented the Left combining with the Right to overthrow Hitler and end the war. It was rubric obsessionalism that split the Christian Church in spite of Christ's warning against division. With only a tenth of the population of Britain members of the Church, they are divided into Protestants and Roman Catholics. And the Protestants, of course, have innumerable divisions.

When the Church was powerful, 'deviationists', however saintly, were burned alive as heretics. Love of God and love of neighbour, the first and great commandments, upon which all the others depend, were an irrelevance. And even to-day attitudes unacceptable to Christ are cultivated in His name. During the Second World War, a large number of Roman Catholic evacuees settled in a part of the country predominantly Protestant. After a discussion between the local vicar and a visiting priest, the astonished vicar complained of condescension. 'Why, he spoke to me as I speak to non-conformist Ministers of religion.' And fresh in our minds are reports of the disruption of family life by a particular sect.

In law, this kind of obsessionalism has led to ridiculous decisions, especially in the part of the law of evidence concerned with hearsay. Almost wherever we look there is fanatical hair-splitting.

Are Christian Pacifists free to support international co-operation based upon goodwill and truth? Will they act on the words of Christ that those who are not against us are for us?

On the threshold of manhood, my left leg was blown off at the thigh on active service. I had had nothing whatsoever to do with war or with politics, national or international. In no way, directly or indirectly, was I responsible for the war. Millions like me have been killed and mutilated in the last fifty years. The omens indicate an earth-wide holocaust. I, a Christian, want to join all who work to prevent it by constitutional means. Would my conscience be at ease were I to join a society of good and able men who, in practice, can do little more than address people of like opinion? Would my conscience be at ease among terrified men, women and children under nuclear bombardment?

The logic of history and Christ's abhorrence of war, war that has, nevertheless, seared Christendom from His day on Earth to this, convince me it is, for me, morally inexcusable to rely upon supernatural intervention to prevent the logical outcome of the continuities in Man.

If, on the other hand, in peace-time, we work together for concerted constitutional action by a Britain united, lifted above the aberrations of Party and careerist politics, and dedicated to establishing the rule of goodwill and truth between all States, we can be assured at least of God's approval in trying to protect the children around us. 'In as much as ye do it unto the least of one of these, my little ones, ye do it unto Me.'

Indeed, as I think of the young mothers and children that nowadays crowd the pavements of our towns and villages, I am loth to make their lives dependent upon my faith. I recall the great faith of Peter. Yet, even his faith wavered, not only when thrice he denied Christ, but also when he trod on the waters and began to sink for the lack of sustained faith. Which of us would have followed Christ after his arrest? How many of us would have run for our lives with the other disciples? Which of us would have had the faith of Peter to step out of the boat at all?

14

Since it is pure faith and love that can perform miracles, I have no right to behave as though I possess them.

Surely, it would be better for pacifists of all kinds to work with anyone and everyone in peace-time for a National Government committed to survival through goodwill and truth for all States.

In the *History of English Law*, Pollock and Maitland write: 'Such is the unity of all history that anyone who endeavours to tell a piece of it must feel that his first sentence tears a seamless web.' Notwithstanding the elegance of this opening sentence, it is probable we have all been helped in our study of history by the convenient but elastic Periods: Ancient, Medieval, Modern and Contemporary.

To round them off, another may be added: the Final; for the end of history is in sight unless spiritual values take over control. This is shown by a glance at the continuities in men throughout recorded history.

The form of an equation may help—

$$
\begin{aligned}
&\text{Intelligence} + \text{Fear} + \text{Self-preservation} \\
&+ \text{Aggression} + \text{Recklessness} \\
&+ \text{Acquisitiveness} + \text{Cruelty} \\
&+ \text{Power} - \text{Goodwill} - \text{Truth}
\end{aligned}
\quad = \quad
\begin{aligned}
&\text{War and Rumours} \\
&\text{of War}
\end{aligned}
$$

After the First World War, after Manchuria, Abyssinia, Resurgent Germany, the Spanish Civil War, the Second World War, Korea, French Indo-China, French North Africa, Suez, the Middle East, Tibet, India, Indo-China again, Cuba and the Congo, can it be seriously argued that Man, unlike the Leopard, has changed his spots?

Yet, statesmen and peoples earnestly intended to make the First World War the war to end wars. Party Politics defeated them, this time, American. In doing so, they unwittingly made possible all the wars that followed. It is agonising to recall a conversation with the eminent American Jurist, Manley Hudson, who told me that ninety per cent. thinking Americans favoured joining the League of Nations. Alas, only ten per cent. were thinking.

15

Can it be argued that men are less cruel after the gas-chambers and concentration camps of Germany; after the treatment of prisoners of war by the Japanese; the treatment of the afflicted survivors of Hiroshima and Nagasaki; the atrocities in South Vietnam and in the Congo, not to mention Apartheid and the manner of its enforcement?

In the more or less recent past, reports of atrocities were softened to fables: there was shame in the world. In the period, Final, so dulled are the sensibilities of the quiescent sophisticated peoples that films of men being whipped to death are shown on television screens in millions of homes, and newspapers exhibit torture in operation. I wonder what effect camera operators had upon those undergoing torture and upon those trussed up awaiting their turn? Any protests by the Governments of Christendom? Any responsibility? Any crowded meetings in the Albert Hall, The Free Trade Hall, St. George's Hall? Any in Cardiff, Aberystwyth, Caernarfon? Any in Aberdeen, Edinburgh, Glasgow? Any in Belfast?

In the first four periods, all the continuities: in the Final, all the continuities plus the return of shamelessness, plus the harnessing of elemental power.

Indeed, again is mankind on the downward path that leads to all they want to avoid. Inspired moral leadership alone can save them. Can the Britain of the 'sixties recapture the spirit of 1940?

One person thinks not—

'This was the last time that London would be the capital of the world. This was an act of mourning for the imperial past. This marked the final act in Britain's greatness. This was a gesture of self-pity, and after this the coldness of reality.'

A more inapposite epitaph cannot be imagined. Yet, these are the words of a columnist who had been given the honour of writing upon Churchill's funeral in a great British newspaper.

The splendour of Churchill's funeral had nothing to do with the grandeur and might of Imperial Britain. It was the

16

poetic expression of an irrepressible surge of gratitude for the moral leadership of 1940. Brute force had brutishly hammered Europe into submission. The oppressed men, women and children of Europe, the threatened men, women and children of Britain and of the world yearned for a Leader who would halt the brute and hurl a defiance whose vehemence and conviction even in 1940 would stir the bells of victory that in 1945 were to resound across the world. Churchill became that Leader. As in 1940, the spirit of Churchill reflected the greatness of Britain, so it reflected the greatness of Britain on Saturday the 30th day of January in the year of our Lord 1965.

Though necessarily complex, the funeral arrangements were so brilliantly conceived, so perfectly performed down to the millionth detail, that I, unlike the columnist, look upon Saturday as an augury of a new age in which a dynamic Britain shall lead the world into an acceptance of the constitutional laws of goodwill and truth that are indispensable to life in the nuclear age.

In establishing these laws of goodwill and truth, women can play a decisive part, and respectfully and hopefully I dedicate this small book to them. If the countries of the world had been governed by women there would never have been any question of nuclear explosions in the atmosphere, in outer space or underground. Women, surely, would never have exposed themselves to the risk of bearing monsters as children; women, surely, would never have taken so dreadful a chance.

May there not be a happy augury in the relatively rare occurrence of a woman being on the throne of Britain in the crucial period when Life itself is in question? Here, already to hand, is a gracious symbol of unity for survival. If each one of us would drop for ten years every issue that divides, and join with everybody else in our country in dedicating himself to the immediate deliverance of Britain from the grave risk of destruction! As we succeeded, so should we save the thousands of millions of pounds a year that are spent over the world on the shocking, degrading and immoral threats of mutilation and butchery of human beings. The whole moral strength of Britain is needed, and in UNITY IS STRENGTH. In a broadcast talk on the 25th of January, 1965, Sir Stephen King-Hall hazarded the guess that were Churchill alive and in his prime, he would go all out for the unity of Britain that rescued civilisation in 1940.

CHAPTER I

THE PENALTY OF APATHY

On the 26th of July, 1945, Churchill and Truman signed this Proclamation to the people of Japan:

> Clause 3. 'The results of the futile and senseless German resistance to the might of the aroused Free Peoples of the World stands forth in awful clarity as an example to the people of Japan.'
>
> Clause 4. 'The time has come for Japan to decide whether she will continue to be controlled by those self-willed militaristic advisers whose unintelligent calculation has brought the Empire of Japan to the threshold of annihilation.'

In other words, under the Law of the Land of every Independent Sovereign State, the Prime Minister of Great Britain and the President of the United States conspired to incite the ordinary people of Japan to commit High Treason! The Prime Minister and the President, of course, were treating the ordinary people as the Political Sovereign Power of Japan—as masters of their own country—in accordance with the political philosophy that places ultimate responsibility for all Acts of State upon the backs of the people.

What response to their proclamation could Churchill and Truman really expect? Did they seriously think the people of Japan would spontaneously rebel and overthrow their government? If, in fact, the people had victoriously rebelled, Hiroshima would never have shattered the tenuous hope of their being somewhere a limit to the frightfulness of Man.

Perhaps Churchill and Truman believed Bertrand Russells sprout from pavements all over Japan! Ought they not, by the way, to have sat beside him? For the casualty list of

Hiroshima is the casualty list of a moment in time of one city, whereas the casualty list of a thermo-nuclear war would be the casualty list of the Earth throughout Time. Also from Potsdam came the following declaration:

'The Allied Armies are in occupation of the whole of Germany, and the German people have begun to atone for the terrible crimes committed under the leadership of those whom, in the hour of success, they openly approved and blindly obeyed.'

Again are the ordinary people held responsible for the crimes conceived, planned, organized and commanded by the legal government of their country, crimes commanded under the threat of a felon's death.

But worse is to come. Apart altogether from the callous strategic considerations foretold by enlightened English minds as the failure the official history has subsequently confirmed, the wholesale bombing of babies, children, women and old people in the crowded working-class areas of Germany was said to be justified as retaliation upon them for their bombing of the towns of Britain. In actual fact, the butchered babies had nothing to do with the bombing of the crowded living-quarters of the poorest and most helpless of the inhabitants of the other side. All this was done by Leaders, who, when successful, attribute responsibility to the survivors of their own frightfulness.

Unless the Code of the Communist World be more ethical than the Code of the ' Free World ', the Communist World must hold responsible the ordinary peoples of the ' Free World ' who allow their respective countries to be used as a nuclear-outpost of the United States. Unfortunately, the Communist belief in the ordinary peoples of the world being the innocent dupes of the Establishments of the ' Free World ', cannot save the ordinary peoples of the West in a nuclear war; for nuclear weapons are no respectors of persons.

Whichever way you look at it, the peoples have to suffer for the moral crimes of their governments. It is vitally important for the peoples to know that the entail of death in every family is the penalty of further crimes; for they must be shaken out of their apathy and aroused to do their duty to themselves and their descendants by trying in the present to understand the basic principles of international politics—

'The foreign policy of any country must be expressive of that country's fundamental national interests.'

This declaration upon foreign policy was broadcast by Secretary of State Cordell Hull on the 12th of September, 1943.

Self-preservation is the most fundamental of all national interests, and every government owes its people all the protection it can provide. This is especially true of the government of the Soviet Union with the wide-open frontiers it has to guard. Especially, after the plunder and scorched-earth devastation by Germany twice in a quarter of a century and the murder of 36,000,000 men, women and children.

In the past, Britannia insisted on a navy big enough to rule the waves because the waves were the approaches to Britain, and when, in the 'thirties, incredibly smug governments neglected to rule the new wide-open approaches of the air, these islands and our way of life came far too near, for our liking, to the fate that overtook England in 1066.

CHAPTER II

BRITAIN: NUCLEAR TARGET NUMBER ONE

As stated in *To Be or Not To Be*, ex-president Eisenhower bids his countrymen beware the 'Military-Scientific Elite' of the United States, and he warns them 'to guard against the acquisition of an unwonted influence, whether sought or unsought, by the Military Industrial Complex', whom I, for convenience and brevity, call the 'Usurpers'.

So in the American booklet, *Community of Fear*, an American professor of Geo-chemistry and a sales consultant, establish the existence in the United States of Supra-constitutional influences dedicated to perpetual hostility to the Soviet Union.

The attitude of these Usurpers placed a heavy legal and moral obligation upon the government of the Soviet Union to bring its defences up to the highest pitch of perfection. They know that while the United States with its one-way Monroe Doctrine has done everything it can to keep away all danger from its own country, it surrounded the Soviet Union with bases for nuclear attack. The air and military marshals of the Soviet Union were, therefore, compelled by military necessity to pin-point on their target-map of defence every one of these nuclear outposts of the hostile United States. The most important? Great Britain.

Because the government, aided and abetted by the Opposition, made Great Britain target number one on the map of defence of the Soviet Union, every second of every minute of every hour of every day, nuclear missiles are poised for flight to Britain, and, notwithstanding Fylingdales, within four minutes of the cataclysmic mistake being made that is certain of being made, Great Britain and its people will be destroyed simply because Britain has allowed herself to be turned into a satellitic outpost of the American Military-Scientific Elite, of the American Military-Industrial Complex : in a word, of the Usurpers.

When the world was brought face to face with a nuclear war over Cuba in October 1962, the American nuclear-submarine depot-ship fled from her moorings in Holy Loch! The people of Britain had to stay where they were, a sitting target for the poised nuclear-missiles of the Soviet Union, a Soviet Union goaded by Americans who, by deliberate act, put us in jeopardy rather than endure the risk to their own country to which for years they have subjected Britain.

The destruction of Great Britain, without any doubt at all, is the inevitable consequence of the subservience to Washington of the British Political Parties.

There is not a moment to lose. Great Britain must be taken off the nuclear-missile target-map of the Soviet Union. But because of the inborn respect for legalism going back centuries, and also because of the long centuries of thinking in terms of world-wide responsibilities, a means of doing so must be found that takes full account of this inherited psychological condition of the people.

In the first book of this trilogy, I try to show the absurdity of partial nuclear disarmament, the impossibility of total nuclear disarmament and the criminal folly of increasing conventional armaments. Indeed, these delusions are so deadly that persistence in them will achieve nothing but time for the nuclear war already at hand.

CHAPTER III

Mewn Undeb y mae Nerth   *Unity is Strength*

THE FIRST ESSENTIAL OF SURVIVAL FOR BRITAIN

GREAT BRITAIN must immediately be removed from the defence map of the Soviet Union.

To do so, the people must be convinced that a subservience that makes us an expendable outpost of the United States is a gross betrayal of the past, present and future of Britain, and of her world-wide responsibilities.

Only a few years ago a person would have been thought insane who prophesised the day was imminent when a British government would voluntarily pursue a policy that in practice gave a foreign newcomer on the European scene the power of life and death over our people even in causes which did not concern us, and to which we might even be opposed.

Are the leaders of all political parties deficient in historical sense? Are they without knowledge and understanding of Constitutional History and Constitutional Law? What other explanation can there be for their overlooking one of the few written basic principles of our unwritten constitution? The principle that denies to foreigners power of decision over war and peace—

> ' In case the Crown and Imperial Dignity of this realm shall hereafter come to any person, not being a native of this realm of England, this nation be not obliged to engage in any war or the defence of any dominions or territories which do not belong to the Crown of England, without the consent of Parliament.' The Act of Settlement.

Perhaps they think the clause has no application where the foreign-born potentate is Head of a foreign state and not of Britain.

24

It is the right of Britain to make herself independent of the will, whim or caprice of any foreigner, and especially of the emotionally imbalanced Usurpers. There should be an immediate end to the cap-in-hand approaches to the Heads of other governments. The voice of Britain should ring out as the voice of Britain, and not as the muffled echo of another country, however affectionately disposed we are to the people of the other country. What I ask for ourselves is nothing more than what they unhesitatingly claim for themselves.

The British people need a government obedient to a people that want to live. It must be provided by constitutional means; for, as already indicated, legalism is an ineradicable part of our national character, a character that would also shrink from any proposal to repudiate the terms implicit in membership of a family of nations.

Self-preservation is as much a fundamental national interest of Britain as it is of the Soviet Union and of the United States of America.

An American programme on Mr. Khrushchev and Berlin, televised by the BBC, sought by suggestion to convince the British people that their long record of high courage guaranteed British support for a foreign policy we know to be American, a policy, for the most part of brinkmanship! I have seen this kind of subtlety goad a moral coward into a fight against his will; but a man who may fear being thought a coward for refusing to accept a personal challenge does not run that risk by refusing to expose helpless children to the horrors of a thermo-nuclear war. In the nuclear-space age, the Briton of highest courage is he who stands by the children and gives single tickets home to American political and military Teddy Boys.

The same programme gave the impression of moral weakness in Italy because of the effect upon its Prime Minister of a visit to Moscow.[1]

[1] Following the subsequent visit to Washington of the Italian Prime Minister, Italy ceased to be an American nuclear-outpost.

If one of you were Head of Government of the Soviet Union, and you knew as a fact your military advisers were morally and legally compelled in defence of their country to plan the destruction of the nuclear outposts of America, what could you do as Head of Government to save the helpless peoples of these outpost countries? Copying Churchill and Truman at Potsdam, you could openly proclaim the fate that would instantly befall the nuclear outposts in the event of the nuclear-war that is the logical and inevitable outcome of brinkmanship in a world of fallible beings.

Khrushchev repeatedly proclaimed this truth, and the inert peoples of the outpost countries joined their Leaders in contemptuously dismissing the warnings as bluff, bullying and blackmail.

If abuse of your solicitude left in your heart any urge to save them, what else could you do? You could invite to Moscow the Prime Minister of one of these countries that he might see for himself the plan to destroy his country simply because it is a nuclear outpost of the United States. Could that Prime Minister honourably expose his country to the certainty of destruction by allowing it to continue an expendable pawn at the mercy of politically immature Usurpers consumed by irrational hate of the Soviet Union? A Prime Minister who knows as a fact there is no question of the Soviet Union wanting to attack any country?

Every reasonably informed person knows the Soviet Union needs peace and the assurance of peace to develop her resources for the benefit of her people. War would destroy all. What she needs, and genuinely wants, is friendship with the United States so that she may throw herself into the life of fulfilment for her people that is possible only in a world at peace engaged predominantly in the arts of peace. This is the explanation of the delight of Mr. Khrushchev with the friendship of Camp David, and of his bewilderment at the betrayal contrived by the Usurpers.[2]

[2] See *To Be or Not To Be.*

Yet speedy co-operation and collaboration between the United States and the Soviet Union is indispensable to life. So true is this that both Leaders owe it to their own countries and to all countries to find some positive way of working together in friendship before the scientists and technologists of other countries become instruments of brinkmanship in the hands of their own variety of supra-constitutional obsessionalists. Those of the United States are more than enough for the good of mankind.

It is because Mr. Khrushchev, spurning personal status and prestige, boldly and insistently pressed for this collaboration that the Usurpers, ' dedicated to perpetual hostility with the Soviet Union ', did every mean thing they could think of to undermine his reputation at home and abroad.

The clear duty of Britain is to promote this friendship. Is she aware of her duty? Has she the moral strength to do so? Is she capable of the impartiality needed? Without impartiality there can be no truth. Without truth there can be no understanding or friendship.

If a Western European capable of reflection were the only survivor of a thermo-nuclear war, what would be the theme of his lamentations?

No thoughts would be wasted upon extinct collossi whose pride lay around him in radio-active dust. Conscience and reason would converge on himself, with a wondering thought upon the quiescence in the ' Free World ' of the vast majority of those who had enjoyed intellectual and moral status.

However, it is answers to the following kind of questions that would consume the twelfth hour. ' Is there any act or omission of mine in this desolate proof of the Fall of Man? ' ' Did I think, did I feel deeply enough, did I feel at all upon the horrors perpetrated by the social, economic, military and political systems of the West of which I was a part? '

Horrors such as the amusement of Italian Pilots at the spectacle of Abyssinians being blown in pieces into the air by the bombs which they themselves had dropped; the

27

razing to the ground of Guernica and Lidice; the dive-bombing of Rotterdam; the gas-chambers for the mass-murder of stripped Jews; Auschwitz and Belsen; the treachery of Pearl Harbour; the treatment of prisoners of war in the hands of the Japanese; the catastrophic omen of Hiroshima and Nagasaki.[3] Duress by the United States could not ease the conscience of a solitary man confronted by death in a wilderness of radio-active dust; he had known all along that the distinction of being the first to explode atomic bombs over men belonged to the United States. They had exploded them over two towns crowded with defenceless babies, children, women and old men. They had proved to the world, and,

---

[3] In a debate in the Second Vatican Council on the passages relating to nuclear weapons in the draft schema de ecclesia, the Melchite Patriarch of Antioch denounced them as unlawful in nature and in no circumstances allowable.

The dogma that at all costs science must progress even though the alleged progress jeopardise all science, knowledge and life is illogical, immoral and insane. For my part, therefore, I have no difficulty in agreeing with the judgment upon scientists that in making elemental power available to nationalist politicians controlled by sectional interests they committed an act unlawful in nature. Men, it is certain, can be saved from the catastrophic consequences of this crime only by moral laws impelled by spiritual power.

With nuclear weapons and space-craft in the hands of human beings who will to practically anything—mental and physical torture is becoming increasingly wide-spread over the world—to further what they regard as their own interests if, in their dim eyes, there seems a reasonable CHANCE of getting away with it without much hurt or loss to themselves, it is obvious the only hope of mankind is in moral laws impelled, as I have said, by spiritual power. The philosophy of the First-Strike strategy of a Nuclear Power against a non-Nuclear Power (Hiroshima and Nagasaki and the reported plan to use ' Nooks ' in Vietnam) exemplifies my proposition. As, of course, does the Second-Strike Strategy by one Nuclear Power against another Nuclear Power (the United States and the Soviet Union).

Is it not ironical that, for the most part, the science and technology that tossed the Bomb into the international arena denies the spiritual Power that alone can neutralise it? What to do with scientists and technologists ought indeed to engage our most earnest attention. In the same debate of the Vatican Council, Archbishop Beck of Liverpool, on the basis of the nuclear weapon having already come into existence, argued that a nuclear weapon is justified if shot into the skies to intercept and destroy a nuclear weapon on its way to mass murder. He is in no doubt, however, that a calculated nuclear attack aimed at killing innocent civilians is murder. This is precisely what took place at Hiroshima and Nagasaki, though Japan had already put out feelers for peace.

28

far worse, to themselves, that no frightfulness is too frightful for contemplation and perpetration by Man.

Convinced, like Al Capone and Hitler, of the efficacy of terror, the Usurpers had threatened a thermo-nuclear war over Berlin—their cherished and vital 'hole in the Iron-Curtain'—and they had very nearly brought it about over Cuba.

The Usurpers, one fears, are far too insensitive to understand that in the nature of things every threat of frightfulness as well as every act of frightfulness is a precedent for the ultimate frightfulness that can have no end.

In this aura of frightfulness, every normal person ought to have foreseen the collision that would one day occur when an inflexible Russian confronted an inflexible American, an American of the charitable faith of a Truman, who believed a benign Providence has made it a law of nature for all Communists to yield at the eleventh hour to the destroyers of Hiroshima and Nagasaki!

Inescapably, the theme of the last lamentation on Earth of the solitary survivor would be the sin of apathy in not having given thought to these things.

I hope there is yet time for each one of us to insure himself against this calamitous guilt: we can begin by thinking and feeling about rights and wrongs. As stated in *To Be or Not To Be*, 'Although I cannot ethically subscribe to the political philosophy that places ultimate responsibility for all Acts of State upon the ordinary people, I do feel that Everyman ought at least to care about what is right and wrong, both in himself and in society. The cumulative effect, at the very least, would be a good climate, and, of course, all kinds of good things can be brought to fruition in a good climate.'

It would help if all the Public Libraries made a point of buying every national political journal in addition to those published in their own areas; for impartial and honest thinking needs the discipline of reading opposing interpretations of the same facts. In this context, it is a comfort to read in the 1962 Commencement Address of President

Deane Malott of Cornell University that 'Cornell must be a place where all points of view are fully expressed and courteously debated.'

What universal freedom and fulfilment, happiness and prosperity there would be if President Deane Malott's words expressed present reality instead of the fine gloss that they are upon the aspirations of Ezra Cornell, the founder of one of America's most dynamic and enlightened Universities![4] Especially if that present reality were of the whole of the United States. Their almost limitless material resources, in subordination to their far greater spiritual potential, would be a joy to the whole world. Certainly, the evil of acquisitiveness that has masqueraded as Generosity and Freedom would disappear. This would also be true of its oppression of peoples who are rising by heroic effort out of an ageless Slough of Despond. So prodigious has been the effort of these peoples, so sustained their patience and forebearance that they will assuredly deserve honourable mention in the story of Man's epic fight with men—if nuclear war is kept at bay.

Returning to conditions as they are and to the possibilities open to you as the humane Head of Government of the Soviet Union, if again your solicitude be disbelieved and disregarded, might not the urgent need of ridding your own country of the menace of satellitic nuclear-bases compel you to give the United States a single dose of her own medicine?

---

[4] On the greatest occasion of his life—inauguration as President after overwhelming electoral success—President Johnson chose to deliver a speech which he himself had prepared. Not for him, on this solemn occasion, the speech of a 'speech-writer'. And not for him an official Bible: he took the oath of President on his mother's Bible.

In the course of his speech he said:

'There are possibilites enough for all who will abandon mastery over others to pursue mastery over nature. There is world enough for all to seek happiness in their own way.'

If I am right in believing there is nothing perfunctory in these words, full value may be given to every one.

This could be done by openly erecting installations for ballistic missiles in Cuba without any attempt at camouflage.[5]

As a startled world saw for itself, the spontaneous reaction of the United States was unilateral action, action that jeopardised the whole of mankind; that brushed aside international law and UNO; that disdained consultation with satellites, euphemistically called allies, every one of which was threatened with destruction simply because the United States was brought within the short-time warning margin to which for years she has subjected so many other countries, including Britain!

The precedent of Cuba has made it more imperative than ever for Britain to remove herself from the defence map of the Soviet Union, before the United States does something that will make the Soviet Union wipe out Great Britain. The dangerous conditions of October 1962 will almost certainly occur again with some other place or occasion the storm centre. Dithering and drifting ensure our annihilation.

The crisis of October 1962 illustrates also the danger of nuclear war that is with us day in day out, the danger of war by accident. With feelings already at fever pitch, an

---

[5] I do not know whether anyone will ever know the Russian motive or motives for sending ballistic missiles to Cuba. As an English judge said in the idiom of his day: ' The thought of Man is not triable: the Devil himself knoweth not the thought of Man.'

However, it is known that at the height of the awesome crisis in October 1962 a note to Washington from Khrushchev broadcast by Radio Moscow contained an offer to trade the missiles in Cuba for American missiles in Turkey. The idea, therefore, was very much in his mind, and this fact remains true even though it be proved that a pledge not to invade Cuba was the only concession made by the United States. It is also true that unprejudiced men and women of reason saw that if the Russians were wrong in installing defensive ballistic missiles in a Cuba that was being constantly threatened by the United States, it was at least as wrong for the United States to install aggressive ones in a Turkey that was being no more threatened than capitalist Finland. Incidentally, this explicit undertaking not to invade Cuba is invaluable for it protects a President of peace from the hysterical demands to invade Cuba that are made intermittently by pressure groups of the Land of the Free who reject as nonsense the claim of Cuba to have freedom of her own.

American U2 flying twelve to thirteen miles high—hostile level—'on a routine sampling mission from Alaska to the North Pole had picked the *wrong star* for its return flight and was at *that moment over the Soviet Union*. Soviet fighter planes had scrambled. American fighters in Alaska had also scrambled and were attempting to rendezvous with the U2 to escort it home'.—Roger Hilsman, American Assistant Secretary of State, in October 1962.[6]

Time being of the essence of our survival, it is the duty of every person to try to think out ways of immediate deliverance for Britain that would honourably take her off the target-map of the Soviet Union. International Conferences galore may be convened when we are honourably safe; but if our deliverance is to depend upon them, our deliverance is postponed for ever. Certainly, in these critical days of inconclusive conferences, Britain must act first and talk afterwards if she is to do her duty to God, to her own people and to the peoples of other lands.

But there is no possibility of independent dynamic action in international affairs under the party political system. Indeed, though believing survival depends upon drastic action, no Party in power would feel so certain of the rightness of its judgment as to act upon it. Moreover, no government would expose itself and its Party to the attacks the Opposition would make inside and outside Parliament, an Opposition, perhaps, genuinely alarmed.

We must have a National Government representative of a whole people aroused to a sense of their imminent peril. A

---

[6] Other incidents of accident: On the 10th of January, 1965, the Polaris-carrying *Ethan Allen* collided with an oil tanker in the Western Mediterranean. So far as I know, it was reported in only one British National Newspaper, and even that newspaper made no further reference to it. A conspiracy of silence! Vital evidence withheld from the people —the Political Sovereign Power responsible for the Acts of its Government!

Similarly, heavily censored was the report of the American Navy upon the total loss in 1963 of the nuclear submarine *Thresher* and of its crew of 195. However, the report of the Congressional Committee on Atomic Energy exposes faults in design and workmanship that would cost £178,000,000 to put right.

government supported by the will to live of all sections of the community, of all age and social levels, all united on our right and will to live.

If the suspense of pre-atomic and pre-nuclear war merged Parties for national survival, as in 1940, so, surely, ought life on the lip of a nuclear volcano in ferment by forces outside our present control.

It is desperately urgent to marshal the moral and intellectual forces of our country that, in practice, waste their energies and opportunities in dispersal of effort. If, for ten years, men and women of all Parties and of no Parties would join together determined to put the survival of life beyond question! Since this can be done without sacrificing the substance of any person's principle, it is plain common sense to put first things first and make sure of the life without which principle can have neither meaning nor future.

If only the Conservative, Liberal and Labour Parties and the Nationalist Parties of Cambria and Scotland would join together for ten years in a National Party! If, for the sake of themselves and of us all, they would postpone proposals that proscribe and divide! I have chosen the word national to emphasize our duty is to the nation, and also to make possible preservation of present Party loyalties by simple hyphenation: National-Labour, National-Liberal, National-Conservative, National-Cambrian, National-Scottish.

It may be thought that as a red rag is to a bull, so is the word National to the Labour Party. But as red qua red has no effect upon a bull for the sufficient reason that bulls are colour-blind, so irrationality may not dominate a Party that is rational. Understanding, however, might be helpful.

Once upon a time—in the pre-nuclear age—Britain was ruled by second-class men who had attracted support by claiming for themselves a monopoly of virtue. Their sense of inferiority kindled jealousy of brilliant predecessors whose co-operation in a coalition government had delivered civilisation from the massive onslaught of the Germans. Having no hope in fair combat, these subtle politicians of second-class minds, denounced coalition as amoral, and they

33

straddled the fairway of Party with postures of high principle! When the fact of coalition became their only salvation, they camouflaged coalition with National Regalia. For this and other reasons in the context of Party, connotations of dishonour are attached to the word national. Now, irrationality plays a bigger part in our lives than we care to admit. A familiar instance is the distaste for ever of some food or drink administered in serious illness. However, though I concede the blight of inhibition from association of ideas, the expulsive power of greater ideas revitalises the freed mind, and the dissipation of the deadly delusions that threaten civilisation presents ideas infinitely greater than the ideas of revulsion for the misdeeds of the past.

For this reason, I feel free to appeal for a pure National Government.

CHAPTER IV

Mewn Undeb y mae Nerth   *Unity is Strength*

BRITAIN'S DUTY: CONCERTED CONSTITUTIONAL ACTION

As long as nuclear war by design is physically possible between nations, nuclear war by accident is inevitable, and if the pre-nuclear mentality and techniques of government persist, we are all doomed.

Up to 1945, laissez-faire, good intentions, self-sacrifice, grand endeavour, noble gestures, civil disobedience, party-political grand inquests, patience, forbearance, departmental routines, with or without hope, either of short-term or long-term effect, often deserved the evoked admiration. In the nuclear-space age, however, they could be catastrophic; for by inducing people to believe there is time for good to fructify, they unwittingly present time to the evil that blights. The indispensable dynamic of life to-day is honest, single-minded, disinterested, dedicated, determination to dissipate the evil in the present.

This can be done if we all unite to work at the highest pressure for a Parliament dedicated to survival.

Bertrand Russell and Canon Collins did their utmost, each in his own way, to awaken people to a sense of imminent peril. The two men and the organisations associated with their names were complementary, and their campaigns attracted the attention of the whole country. In the next chapter, I try to bring out the ethical nature of Bertrand Russell's self-sacrificing work for the survival of Man, Law and Civilisation.

In this chapter, however, I invite Bertrand Russell and Canon Collins and their late colleagues and supporters to bless and support a campaign for a National Parliament that can constitutionally achieve all that they want and very much more. Having already achieved so much in their several ways, may not the moment have come when a concerted campaign to establish a National Parliament might win even more spectacular results?

The urgent need is to attract, retain and give purpose to the people, and, at the same time, keep on active service the talented men and women of conviction, too often wasted in gaol. Gaol accomplished all it can accomplish when it imprisoned the scientist-philosopher who transformed it into a broadcasting house for the propagation of ideas on a wave-length above the reach of warders and scientists in the pay of governments.

The need of dynamic educational work in the minds of all sections of the community was high-lighted by the excitement of all three political Parties over the significance of the result of the by-election at Orpington in between the General Elections of 1959 and 1964. Their behaviour was the antiquated antics of half a century ago that took a future for granted. 'Thou fool, this night thy soul shall be required of thee.' And even the New Statesman used the Front Page to repeat what had already been made crystal clear to millions of viewers. Moreover, in the issue of this journal of the 19th of January, 1962, Muggeridge climbs nimbly up and down three columns and out of sight with the dead weight on his mind of the second volume of *The Concise Dictionary of National Biography*!

However, from the plinth of Nelson's Column—doing his duty for England the more gallantly, for England's not expecting him to do it—in the frosts of a long symbolic winter, the greatest living philosopher in his 90th year, warned the earnest, but pathetically helpless young people before him, of the death that so soon might descend upon them.

When the threat of annihilation is lifted, editors, to their hearts' desire, may entangle themselves and their readers in the colourful yarns that embroider political gossip. For the present, however, may it not be their duty to cut out faded patterns that obscure national vision in the same way as the eye-surgeon cuts out the cataract? May it not be their duty to dedicate their journals to the task of saving humanity by giving to this task more and more space in diminishing time?

Churchill would have towered even over the Churchill we knew if he had prevented the Second World War that he foresaw. In the autumn of 1876, Gladstone published the pamphlet, *The Bulgarian Horrors and the question of the East*, that heralded ' the most famous political campaign ever waged by a popular leader in the annals of English democracy ', to quote Ensor. A few years later came his Midlothian Campaigns. If, day in, day out, the oratory of Churchill had stirred from their torpor the people of Britain, there might have been no Second World War. An aroused Britain would have compelled Chamberlain to welcome the overtures of Washington and Moscow, and the calculating Hitler would almost certainly have yielded to second and wiser thoughts.

Of Chamberlain's need of compulsion, let Churchill speak—

' Mr. Roosevelt was indeed running great risks in his own domestic politics by deliberately involving the United States in the darkening European scene. All the forces of isolationism would have been aroused if any part of these interchanges had transpired. On the other hand, no event could have been more likely to stave off, or even prevent, war than the arrival of the United States in the circle of European hates and fears. To Britain it was a matter of life and death. No one can measure in retrospect its effect upon the course of events in Austria and later at Munich. We must regard its rejection—for such it was—as the loss of the last frail chance to save the world from tyranny otherwise than by war. That Mr Chamberlain, with his limited outlook and inexperience of the European scene, should have possessed the self-sufficiency to wave away the proffered hand stretched out across the Atlantic leaves one, even at this late date, breathless with amazement. The lack of all sense of proportion, and even of self-preservation, which this episode reveals in an upright, competent, well-meaning man, charged with the destinies of our country and all who depended upon it, is appalling. One cannot today even reconstruct that state of mind which would render such gestures possible.

'I have yet to unfold the story of the treatment of the Russian offers of collaboration in the advent of Munich. If only the British people could have known and realised that, having neglected our defences and sought to diminish the defences of France, we were now disengaging ourselves, one after the other, from the two mighty nations whose extreme efforts were needed to save our lives and their own, history might have taken a different turn. But all seemed so easy from day to day. Now, ten years later, let the lessons of the past be a guide.'

If Churchill, in the 'thirties, had thrown himself into a campaign of peace with the same surpassing devotion, energy and conviction that he gave to the campaign of war, he might have prevented the Second World War. If he had prevented the Second World War by having Chamberlain blown, either out of office, or into the arms of the United States, the Soviet Union and France, the precedent of working together for self-preservation might have elevated co-operation and collaboration between the four into a rule of law so strong that peace on earth would have been at long last assured.

The fateful events chronicled by Churchill are of the 'thirties. Have the lessons of three ten-year periods been a guide? Consider the Party Leader, Anthony Eden, the best qualified in Foreign Affairs of any Party Leader at any time: yet in Foreign Affairs he was a dismal failure when Prime Minister.

To-day, when the mistakes of a Chamberlain or an Eden could mean irremediable catastrophe to human life and civilisation, we dare not gamble upon Party Leaders.

Yet, in Britain, where, in the periods of preparation for war—the periods called peace, when, first, we lick our wounds and then prepare for more—Party politics are accepted as the highest form of government. Notwithstanding the grave consequences of notorious neglect, which we, belatedly united, feverishly had to correct at considerable cost and peril in the two world wars! Without any doubt at all, to-day, the consequence of failure ' in peace ' is the end of everyone. Where Party comes first, as first it will come in Party politics, failure is certain.

CHAPTER V

Mewn Undeb y mae Nerth   *Unity is Strength*

THE PHILOSOPHY OF BERTRAND RUSSELL'S CIVIL DISOBEDIENCE

WHEN, over and over again, crimes of the same pattern are perpetrated by a gang, the police instinctively hunt the master-criminal who weaves the pattern and who dominates the gang.

It was as well known to the police as it was to the vast majority of the people that the master-mind of the Committee of One Hundred was Bertrand Russell, and, as he made no secret either of his identity or of his activities, so did he make no secret of his address. Indeed, his crimes blossomed in the open, and, stranger still, arrest and trial emblazed with light the convictions that drove him, a light refracted to the four quarters of a sympathetic world by the four walls of the prison intended to extinguish it. An insoluble problem for the authorities.

Must not effects like these emanate from intentions of superlative good? The unpleasantness of sitting on pavements for the future of others and not of himself underlines the thought. Many will endure hardship in the present to ensure for themselves a secure future; but here is a man in his ninetieth year who risked his life for the future of others. Most people share Pascal's respect for testimony that may cost the witness his life. How much greater the respect when the witness is the world's greatest living philosopher, who teaches that because ' . . . respect for law is an indispensable condition for the existence of any tolerable social order ', no man is right in going outside the ways provided by the constitution for changing a law ethically bad except ' . . . when a man profoundly believes it would be a sin to obey '.

39

How much more justified is such a man when no constitutional means of practical value exist! Bertrand Russell profoundly believed the nuclear policy of the great political Parties was heading inevitably to the destruction of society, civilisation and mankind. Further, he believed this catastrophe could overtake us before the term of office of the government expired. To wait for the General Parliamentary Election, therefore, was to run the risk of waiting for our doom. But no Parliamentary Election upon the supreme issue of Life or Death seemed likely at any time; for in essentials, the three great Parties shared the same policy. Thus, any Back-bencher who opposed the Government on this issue, opposed *ipso fact* the official Opposition, and ran the risk of political extinction through expulsion from his Party—Labour or Conservative.

In these circumstances, how could Bertrand Russell get across to the ordinary people the reality of their imminent peril? Since, in practice, there was no consitutional way open to him to reach out into the homes of the people, ought he to have bowed his head in resignation as a law-abiding citizen? Ought he to have done nothing of practical value to avert the destruction of Great Britain and its 53,000,000 inhabitants? It is because this man, already renowned, believed the physically easy and comfortable course would have amounted to the wrong of betraying his country that he and his followers quickened the pillory of pavements and courts into Parliaments of survival.

Incidentally, who is the friend of law, the one who does nothing to avert desolation and chaos that are the negation of law, or the one who temporarily and non-violently disobeys a minor law in order to ensure the Rule of Law for ever? Bertrand Russell sat on pavements to save Law and Civilisation.

It may also give understanding to well-meaning people who interminably ask disciplined people sitting quietly on cold pavements whether they like law-breaking, if I direct their attention to the Science of Ethics by Sir Leslie Stevens.

Admitting the undoubted fact that in Britain the King in Parliament can legally make and unmake any law, and that in the eyes of the courts no other authority may disregard or supersede any enactment of the King in Parliament, Stevens goes on to say that subjects, nevertheless, would be idiotic who submitted to an Act of Parliament that ordered the murder of blue-eyed babies.

Do you not agree with Stevens?

If you would raise your voice against the murder of blue-eyed babies, would you not raise your voice against the murder of all babies? Would you think twice of sitting on pavements if sitting on pavements were the surest, if not the only, way of informing lethargic parents of the imminent peril to their children? Who is the idiot, the person who warns the parents in the only certain way open to him of the fate prepared for their children or the person who gapes? And who are the parents? The parents are the Political Sovereign Power of Great Britain whose will, political philosophers tell us, is the ultimate power in the land. Readers of John Austin will recall that he makes even legal sovereignty reside in the electoral body of the Commons together with the King and the Peers: to him, the Commons are the trustees of the electors. All that Bertrand Russell did was to do non-violently everything in his power, however dangerous to his health, to get the electors to inform their trustees that because of their wish and will to live, they renounce nuclear weapons.

But he did more than sit on pavements. He wrote books and articles and travelled long distances to make speeches. Were not these efforts, prodigious even for a man in physical prime, sufficient to convince him he had done all that could reasonably be expected? Notwithstanding the clearest of minds, intent upon making every word speak, he must have known that whereas only a fraction of the population either read his books and articles or attend his meetings, there is no one, literate or illiterate, who does not know our foremost philosopher sits on pavements because he desperately wants the people to know the policies of the politicians of the West—the policies for which we, the sovereign political power of Britain, are responsible—are orientated to nuclear war and death.

Surely, appealing, lamb-like, but in the most effectual way open to him, direct to the lethargic Political Sovereign People to heed his warnings of the approaching holocaust, did not make him a law-breaker in anything but a technical sense. I am sure that when the day of doom dawns and dissipates all deadly delusions, those who have condemned our Premier Philosopher for sitting on pavements, will condemn our Premier Politician for not having done so too.

Finally, I draw your attention to Eichman. The elimination of Jews was the deliberate policy of the supreme authority in Germany, a supreme authority recognized by every other Independent Sovereign State as having full legal power within the frontiers of Germany. Without any doubt at all, Eichman acted in accord and in accordance with the will of those whose word was Law in the Germany of those days.

Later, another Independent Sovereign State, in physical possession of alien Eichman, condemned him to death for acts done in his own country under the orders of his own supreme legal authority.

What was the nature of the authority under which the judges condemned Eichman? The Law in Israel.

So far as law itself is concerned, the law under which Eichman acted was a law applied to the citizens of Germany living in Germany, whereas the law applied by the judges in Israel was a law applied to a foreigner illegally abducted from a third Independent Sovereign State. Therefore, there was more legality on the side of Germany than on the side of Israel. Legality! The legality of the particular acts of the German Independent Sovereign State excites the disgust and condemnation of every civilised human being, whereas the dignity, patience and fairness of the trial of Eichman excite the admiration of the world.

In other words, though in an Independent Sovereign State, the judges have no authority to act on any principle outside the law of the land they were appointed and paid to administer, the law they do administer can be devoid of ethical content. The law that countenanced the execution of 6,000,000 Jews because they were Jews had no ethical content.

The case of Eichman and the trials of Nuremberg exemplify the intrinsic inferiority of a man-made law that transgresses the moral law. One feels, however, that disinterested parties are the Parties best qualified to administer the Moral Law. However fair the trials at Nuremberg, a better and a safer precedent would have been established if prosecuting counsel and the judges had been drawn exclusively from neutral countries, and if all combatants— the defeated as well as the victors—had been free to submit charges to a neutral grand jury that could impartially determine whether a *prima facie* case of unconscionable conduct had been made out.

For instance, Germany might have wished to prosecute the United States and Great Britain for the unnecessary suffering inflicted by their insistence on unconditional surrender. And Japan might have wished to prosecute the United States for the frightfulness of Hiroshima and Nagasaki.

It appears, after all, that the two world wars have not destroyed the philosophy of Might being Right. Indeed, the Usurpers of the United States act unashamedly on the principle of Might being the supreme arbiter between right and wrong: hence their insistence upon our doing what we are told! Hence their insistence, too, upon the exclusion from the United Nations of the People's Republic of China.

Though you will have seen that I do not fit into the category of either unilateralist or multilateralist, and that legalism is in my bones, yet fairness and respect for men of conviction compel me to invite those scornful of Bertrand

43

Russell, and of the young people who flocked to his banner, to ponder upon these words of our own great Blackstone—

'The Law of Nature being coeval with mankind, and dictated by God Himself, is, of course, superior in obligation to any other. It is binding over all the Globe, in all countries and at all times: no human laws are of any validity if contrary to this; and such of them as are valid derive all their force and all their authority, mediately or immediately, from this original.'

The Law of Nature condemns nuclear war and the suicide of Man.

To-day, of course, there is no such juristic opinion, and as I have already indicated, judges are not free to consider any law that is not allowed for by the law of their own Independent Sovereign State. Nevertheless, goodness, self-preservation and the preservation of his fellow-citizens and, indeed, of his rulers may require a citizen more perspicacious than his rulers to disobey his rulers.

An engine-driver of a midnight crowded passenger train absent-mindedly drives past a signal showing red at seventy miles and hour. The stoker tells him to stop. It is the duty of the driver to command. It is also his duty to use his own judgment and certainly he may not act on the judgment of a subordinate. Accordingly, he tells the stoker to stoke and mind his own business. Ought the stoker to obey or disobey? Ought he to do everything in his power to save the lives of hundreds of passengers by stopping the train or ought he to mind his own business of stoking? If the passengers knew of their peril, what would they wish the stoker to do? The passengers to a man would want the stoker to disobey his superior in the same way as Churchill and Truman wanted the people of Japan to disobey their rulers even in time of war.

Because the sovereign power of a State is exercised by human beings occasions will inevitably arise when those human beings are either evil or unequal to the responsibilities of government. If obedience to these people involve serious wrongdoing to others, the moral law may call for disobedience. Hence the Proclamation to the people of Japan by Churchill and Truman. Hence the condemnation and execution of Eichman. Hence the trial of senior Nazis.

In the well-considered judgment of our greatest philosopher, the policy of all three political parties in Britain is heading inevitably to the destruction of Britain and the extinction of Man. If this be true, his advocacy of very occasional meek civil disobedience was surely more justified than Churchill's and Truman's threats to make the people of Japan commit High Treason.

The organs of publicity being almost wholly subject to the influence of the immovable Establishment, impressing his body on the pavements of London has been more effectual than his speeches and books in impressing his views on the minds of the people.

I hope the trouble I have taken to explain Bertrand Russell's Civil Disobedience will put an end to the cheap jibes that have been made by citizens of exemplary character, intelligence and learning, who ought to have known better.

The history books will enlighten those who may still be in doubt upon the problem of God and conscience versus State. An obvious instance is the conflict between Church and State from the time of Constantine onwards.

CHAPTER VI

Mewn Undeb y mae Nerth   *Unity is Strength*

INTERNATIONAL CO-OPERATION AND COLLABORATION IN SCIENCE MUST SUPPLANT COMPETITION

IN Party politics, for Party purposes, the Leader of the Opposition is expected to exploit every discomfiture of the government of the day, and no Leader dare fall far short of expectations. Careerist no less than Party interests so crystallize Party consciousness that any plea for a National Government makes no impact on the Headquarters of Party. Hence the need of this direct appeal to the Sovereign Political Power of Britain : the electorate itself.

When thousands of nuclear weapons in the West poised for the East, and thousands of nuclear weapons in the East poised for the West, might be detonated by accident or design over Berlin, Cuba, Indo-China or the like, it is surely wrong for the political leaders of the oldest democracy in the world to be compelled by the Party system to engage in petty squabbling.

A grave problem demanding immediate solution is the control of scientists and technologists in the pay of wealthy governments eager to lavish thousands of millions of pounds a year upon works of destruction. The prestige race to the moon supplied the code word: lunacy.[1] The inescapable consequence of Campaign Lunacy is the extinction of Man.

[1] In his Christmas message on the 22nd of December, 1964, the Pope described nationalism as the first of the elements that oppose the development of human brotherhood, and he pleaded for control of the ythal spirit of rivalry and prestige.

46

As stated in Appendix Three of *The Soviet Union: Another Look*, Sir William le gros Clark said in his Presidential Address to the British Association in 1961: the exploitation of science in power politics threatens the extinction of Man; that International Co-operation must supplant International Competition; that the dangers are formidable and that time is getting short.

International Co-operation must supplant International Competition!

But how can this be done while well-paid Scientists and Technologists work exclusively for hostile states striken with jealousy and distrust?[2] All, ostensibly, on the issue of opposing idealogical principles inherited by peoples who had nothing to do either with their creation or reception, and who are powerless to change them. In any case, such evils as exist under Capitalism or Communism are heaven compared to the evils prepared by scientists and technologists. Undoubtedly, the supreme issue is what to do with lavishly endowed competitive science. ' Co-operation must supplant competition.' A means must be found. A beginning must be made by some country. Great Britain can make that beginning herself. ' The dangers are formidable, and time is getting short.' Certainly, there is no time for Party squabbling.

In case the warnings of a President of the British Association be insufficient to awaken the people to a sense, alike of awful peril and great opportunity, I repeat a similar warning by Schweitzer: ' Man has lost his capacity to foresee and to forestall, he will end by destroying the Earth.'

Then is the doom of Man inevitable? It would, indeed, be inevitable if the Establishments of the World constituted the whole of Man. Fortunately, they do not. Indeed, they are a tiny fraction of the whole, and the deliverance of Man is indeed possible if individual men and women take up at long last their individual and inalienable duty.

[2] Senator Barry Goldwater believed he enhanced his prospects of victory in the Presidential election by advocating the breaking off of diplomatic relations with the Soviet Union!

I am afraid the awe of laymen, and the questions put to scientists by interviewers and reporters upon subjects about which scientists as scientists know nothing, have the dangerous effect of stimulating narcissistic neurosis.[3] Every scientist might gain a sense of proportion by submitting to the self-discipline of trying every morning to pin-point his speck of knowledge in the chart of omniscience, and, in particular, any discovery that he himself has made.

However, mechanistic their view of the world, I am more than willing to listen with humility to anything said upon the specialist work of scientists evolved by the Doctrinaires of Determinism; but I am not prepared to hear them as scientists authoritatively dismiss precious beliefs about which science knows nothing at all. In common with all citizens in these days of tolerance, scientists as citizens are free to accept or reject Theism: their status of scientist, however, adds not a whit to the credibility of either theism or atheism.

The unceremonious dismissal of God by distinguished scientists acutely distresses people of simple faith. Of course, if the scientist, as a scientist, could prove there is no God, a defence could be made of his ruthlessness: since he cannot, let him respect and reverence the peace of mind of the people who do believe.

It would also be proper for him to reflect upon the willing service rendered by Ministers of Religion to people stricken by illness, disablement, bereavement or loneliness. Has he

[3] Addressing a meeting in Montreal of the American Association for the Advancement of Science on the subject of ethics in science, Professor Barry Commoner of Washington University, St. Louis, listed influences that are making for a breakdown in scientific integrity. The instances given include political and military pressures, research and space-craft competition.

An amazing revelation is that scientists (as a class, so boastful of accuracy and certainty) failed to take account of the radioactivity in plants and animals in their report to the Atomic Energy Commission of the United States, upon the hazards of fall-out in the 1950s. (See *The Times*, 5/1/1965.)

given a thought to the effect of uncertainty upon the minds of people who are worried by their apparent inability to halt the threat of nuclear war, by mysterious illnesses, by deformities and by the increasing number of people who suffer from leukemia? Whatever officialdom says, these happenings are connected in the peoples' minds with radioactive fall-out, and with the unregulated and widespread use of insecticides and weed-killers of ever increasing toxicity. Has he given a thought to the relationship between these anxieties and the large number of hospital-beds occupied by mental patients? The scientist ought to be the last person to undermine the spiritual foundation of the Church, whose poorly-paid incumbents are so often called upon to minister to men and women afflicted in body and mind by the evil things let loose by the affluent destroyers of physical and mental health.

Latterly, however, I have wondered whether there is justification for amazement at the insensitivity of atheistic scientists engaged in work for mass-destruction. Three great men come to mind who argue trenchantly upon the inadequacy of reason in human behaviour: St. Paul, Spinoza and our own Locke.

If reason cannot be relied upon, and spiritual sanctions have no application, what check is there upon the activities of scientists? None. Neither Positive Law nor the omnibus rule of good behaviour enjoined by Public Opinion is concerned with the nature of the work done by scientists, however lethal its ultimate effect.

In February 1963, upon the theme of pest-destroying and weed-killing, two books were published in the United States. One, significantly named, *Silent Spring*, is by Rachel Carson, a biologist and writer of international repute. The other, *Our Synthetic Environment*, is by Lewis Herber, a journalist.

Agreement from the Right, Centre and Left is both significant and re-assuring.

The Critic of the Conservative Newspaper:

'They constitute a most terrifying document.

' The only remedy I can see is a non-profit-making authority in charge of the ecology of the planet which will undertake the protection of the harmless birds, fishes, animals, plants and insects which are being exterminated by the commercial chemical firms and their products; and defend us from by-products which are poisoning Man.'

The Critic of the Independent Newspaper:

' How is it that this threat has come about? Largely because of ignorance, insufficient fundamental research, complacency, vested interests and lack of public awareness.

' Some scientists in high places in both industry and government make a grave mistake, primarily, I believe, because most of them are narrowly trained as chemists and have no knowledge or comprehension of the incredibly complex interrelations and interactions of living things. With these new chemical weapons of mass murder the danger-point can be overstepped with terrifying ease.'

The Critic of the Journal of the Left:

' In Silent Spring, she has set out, on the basis of thorough investigation and documentation, to estimate and protest against the hideous damage to life in general done by the alliance between government agencies, pest-control organisations, farmers and chemical manufacturers ruthlessly on the make, to wipe out whole races of creatures which, either directly by eating crops, or indirectly as vectors of pathogens, are troublesome to Man.'

A terrifying document indeed, to quote the Critic of the Conservative Newspaper. An indictment prepared by public spirited private citizens. Where are the public spirited statesmen, politicians, civil servants and scientists? And all well paid. On the evidence before us, are these the kind of people we can depend upon with certainty to safeguard our lives against the misuse of nuclear-weapons and space-craft?

God and spirituality out of the way, and the grateful laity emancipated from the ' Terror of the Supernatural ', these

50

modern DDs (Doctrinaires of Determinism), on the one hand, harness elemental power calculated to terrify all the peoples of the world, and, on the other hand, scatter poisons over our fertile earth that destroy everything except the insects they were intended to destroy.[4]

The paramount and urgent need indeed is a philosopher-supervised International State for all scientists and technologists engaged in work that in the competitive world deplored by Sir Wilfrid le gros Clark is a ruthless killer.

Because international conferences consume the time it is imperative to save, a beginning must be made by a country of dogged determination with traditions and experience of ' going it alone '.

To ensure victory, in 1940 Britain welded together as one nation. To-day, present peace of mind, astronomical sums of money, the achievements of all the centuries that have been handed down to us for safekeeping, development and bequest, demand a united nation of one mind bent upon one thing: control of the elemental power science and technology have put at the disposal of nations morally and intellectually unfit to possess it.

But is it realistic to expect a Party to forfeit prospects of Party electoral success? Is it realistic to deny Party Leaders the ambition of presiding over Whitehall? I counter these anachronistic questions with another. How long shall we be here to indulge in Party Warfare? And there is another, how long shall we deserve to be here?

Though ' Mankind cannot bear very much reality ' (Eliot), statesmen must face the fact that in the very present, in the name of a deterrent that cannot deter, thousands of millions of pounds are being spent annually over the world upon weapons capable of destroying all life. It is the inescapable

---

[4] From experiments made by the United States Department of the Interior, DDT has been discovered in the bodies of penguins and seals that have never left the Antarctic; and world-wide contamination by this pesticide is feared. The specimens containing the minute traces of DDT were collected from the Antarctic in February 1964.

duty of statesmen to act on the assumption that, in the hands of bitter enemies, weapons that can destroy all life will destroy all life.

Until this absolute duty is successfully discharged there is no time or place in Great Britain for either personal or party ambitions.

Statesmen would be gravely at fault to let events drift because some well-informed well-meaning people believe that although there is nothing that men can do to prevent a thermo-nuclear war, they need not despair of Life itself because only hundreds of millions of people will be destroyed outright! There was a great deal of confident, academic and objective appraisal of the Maginot Line: how false facts were to show it to be!

I write because I believe a thermo-nuclear war can be prevented by the dynamic Britain symbolised in the two World Wars by Lloyd-George and Churchill. Without such a Britain I believe there will be a nuclear war.

In this awful context, first things must surely come first for statesmen as for us all.

CHAPTER VII

Mewn Undeb y mae Nerth   *Unity is Strength*

THE MIXED-MANNED NAVAL FORCE

THE Mixed-Manned Naval Force, a Washington-Bonn hybrid, was the spurious symbol of nuclear status offered to non-communist aspirants of nuclear honours to discourage them from making nuclear weapons of their own. They were to be content with subscribing to the capital and maintenance costs of naval surface ships fitted with American-made Polaris nuclear-rockets, and to send their quota of sailors to man the ships. They were also to be given the privilege of subscribing to the capital costs of the rockets.

West Germany, for the present, welcomes any plan that, in practice, will accustom the world to the fact of Germany being publicly associated with nuclear weapons.[1] After all, one thing leads to another, and small beginnings have a way of developing. Already a Secretary of State speaks of West Germany as America's main partner in NATO![2]

Without the ulterior motives of West Germany, France and Britain opposed the scheme; France, firmly; Britain, ditheringly.

---

[1] 'The Federal Chancellor declares that the Federal Republic undertakes not to manufacture in its territory any atomic weapons, chemical or biological weapons.' (Annex I to Protocol No. III on the Control of Armaments under the Brussels Treaty of March 17, 1948, Bundesgesetzblatt 1955. Nr. 7. Bonn, March 25, 1955.)

It is important to take note of the fact that the declaration excludes only the making of these weapons by the Federal Republic within her own territory. It does not exclude Germany from making them in other countries or of other countries making them in Germany, and the declaration does not renounce the possession or the use of nuclear weapons.

[2] See Dean Rusk's speech delivered in Frankfurt on the 27th of October, 1963, at the inauguration of a memorial to the late General Marshall. An important German objective.

Britain dithered because she did not feel free. Long years of submission to the United States has made it difficult for Britain to do anything but nod or shake her head in re-active response to the will of Washington. Basically, this was the cause of the confusion of Macmillan, and of the associated 'British Sickness' that De Gaulle felt compelled to keep at arm's length.

Enjoying her hegemony, the Land of the Free, the Land of the Monroe Doctrine presented to Britain the ultimatum: 'Either you join the mixed-manned force or we, and our main partner in NATO—Germany, will go on without you.' A partnership of America and Germany upon the waves! The waves upon which Britain depends for her existence.

Add to this insensitivity of our sensitive Ally, the heavy and widespread increase of vested interest in world division, and the evil nature of the monster becomes evident. In our day, whether we like it or not, elemental power makes love of neighbour obligatory upon everybody. To-day, truly, every man is his brother's keeper. In submission to the spirit of the Christian Church, is it too much to ask of statesmen who publicly observe its rites, to act upon a fundamental law of Christ that scientists themselves have made mandatory in the present?

Misgivings are also excited by the vulnerability of these surface ships however deceitfully camouflaged as ordinary merchantmen. Even if manned vehicles like the British TSR-2 or a substitute capable of delivering with precision either conventional or nuclear weapons, tactical or strategic, could or would be used against war-ships, the known practice of deception would extinguish all hope of discrimination. Perhaps I am being absurdly academic or naïve. After all, in the First and Second World Wars, the U-boats of the 'main partner of the United States in NATO' gave enthusiastic priority to defenceless merchantmen. For the First World War, let the *Lusitania* speak; for the Second, the *Athenia*.

It is no wish of mine to rivet Germany to her past, and in *The Soviet Union: Another Look* I suggest she become an equal member with us of the British Commonwealth of Nations. Alongside us, Germany would have an ally capable of overcoming the indefinable something in a regimented Germany that in a single generation twice erupted into World War. Because of the horror of a Third World War, no moral person either inside or outside Germany dare say with certainty that that indefinable something has been eradicated. For the safety of herself no less than for that of the world, Germany needs a close political partner with the will and the means to provide a spiritual counterpoise to violence.

I do not believe she will be given that spiritual counter-poise in close partnership with the United States. Notwith-standing fear of the Usurpers, no one who has read *To Be or Not To Be* can doubt the genuineness of my affection for the people of the United States: neither can they question my hope of their great country being led by great Presidents. Nevertheless, to me the ruthlessness of the powerful Usurpers at work on the peculiar malleability of German mentality makes a terrifying prospect.

If there is to be a close partnership between Germany and another country, I am certain it would be better for Germany, Eastern Europe and the world for that close partnership to be with Britain. If there is to be a close partnership between the United States and another country of the West, it would be better for the world, as it would be for the United States, for that close partnership to be with Britain. Provided always the Government of Britain be a National Government representative of a people as determined in the 'sixties upon peace and survival as they were upon victory when they stood alone in 1940.

Returning to the idea of the M.L.F. we see hypocrisy and naiveté. It was hypocritical for pretending to change what was never intended to be changed: it was naïve for trying to deceive any country, and no self-respecting country of pure motive would have joined it voluntarily.

Independently of the fundamental wrongness of the scheme, however, was it ever workable?

In every ship there is to be a contingent of superior beings in exclusive control of the nuclear rockets. However tactful the American contingents, however restrained American exuberance, the bare fact of their exclusive control of the weapon that is the *raison d'etre* of the ship must set them apart and above all other nationals on board, in their own eyes as well as in the eyes of the others. Apartheid at sea!

Now, for centuries British sailors have ranked with the best in the world. Is it psychologically possible for them to be content on board a ship in which they are inferior for being British?

When British physicists took their advanced knowledge to the United States during the Second World War because of the vulnerability of Britain, and in collaboration with others made possible the atomic and nuclear weapon, did they dream the United States would degrade the British nation and sailor with the power thus derived? If the British contribution to the atomic and nuclear pools of knowledge be minimised to thimblefulls, is the communication to the United States of our advanced radar knowledge also held negligible? And when Britain freely gave the formula of life-saving penicillin, did any Briton expect to pay tribute to American manufacturers? Is genius nothing and technology everything?

I think it reasonable to say that branded and disgruntled national sections are unlikely to weld into a homogeneous Ship's Company.

CHAPTER VIII

Mewn Undeb y mae Nerth   *Unity is Strength*

THE NUCLEAR PROBLEM POSED

IF a National Government dedicated to the preservation of Man and civilisation came into being in Britain, hope would re-charge the human heart.

Provided goodwill and truth for all nations were seen to be and were known to be the unchanging ideal of the British Parliament and Government, this hope would never falter however short of perfection particular proposals might be.

Without any doubt at all, we must go all out to make impossible the Third World War and to end the shame of spending thousands of millions of pounds upon weapons designed to butcher human beings. It is impossible to go all out with one mind expect as one nation: the job calls for one mind.

In the years that preceded 1914, there were influential people in Britain who refused to believe a ' scrap-of-paper ' mentality ruled Germany. Notwithstanding the grim lesson of the First World War and the omens that darkened the 'thirties, incredibly, there were again in Britain influential people who refused to acknowledge the same inalienable entail. From a window in Downing Street waving, for a second time that day, the joint declaration of himself and Hitler, Chamberlain said: ' This is the second time in our history that there has come back from Germany to Downing Street peace with honour. I believe it is peace for our time.' And to the last moment, almost, one of our national newspapers screamed there would be no war.

Because there are in existence at the disposal of very fallible human beings nuclear weapons capable of destroying all life, no sane person has the right to say they will never be used. Because it is impossible to be certain there will be no nuclear war in a divided world, he who says so deepens the apathy of people already in it up to their armpits.

It is, therefore, peculiarly distressing to find one of the most equable and enlightened professors of history in the English-speaking world equating parity with peace between the nuclear powers. How deadly the delusion! How fallacious the argument! Strangely enough, almost in the same breath, the view of Paul Valéry is accepted of 'outcome' in history falsifying all predictions and betraying all expectations. Betrayal of the professor's expectations means a nuclear war and the END of Man!

If history showed morals and reason invariably triumphant, justification might have to be conceded. But, as we have just seen, the lack of them in the 'thirties made Churchill, even in the later forties, 'breathless with amazement'. Did reason prevail in the fiasco of Suez when Anthony Eden wore the mantle of Prime Minister? And, on paper, Anthony Eden was the best qualified in Foreign Affairs of any Party Leader we have ever had. Especially on the Middle East.

On the question of morals in International Affairs, I direct the attention of the professor to the footnote on page 82 of *To Be or Not To Be.*

In so far as the professor relies upon fear and self-preservation, where is the conclusive evidence that they invariably deter? In the nuclear-space age, the evidence has to be conclusive and the deterrent absolute. To prove there is no such evidence to sustain the professor's dangerous assumption, it is sufficient to refer to the well-established condition of mind that does not advert either to self or to penalty. For instance, recklessness. There is also the condition of mind aware of both, that acts on the assumption of escape by cleverness or 'muddling through'! Conditions of mind upon which the Establishment specialises.

In so far as the professor's thesis depends upon invariable obedience, carefulness and efficiency by subordinates, where is the conclusive evidence required? I point to the shot-down U2 of Pilot Powers, discussed on pages 57 and 78 of *To Be or Not To Be*; to the incident of jet aeroplanes made in France on licence for Belgium, flown into Katanga by pilots of the United States of America against the will of the President (the pilots were punished). This incident is also discussed in the same book on page 125. For instances of mistake, see my quotation of Roger Hilsman, American Assistant Secretary of State in October 1962, given in chapter 3 of this book. See also the footnote.

For the meaning and irrelevance of 'parity' between one nuclear State and another, I direct attention to chapter 11 of this book on French and American Psychoneurosis, and to page 151 of *To Be or Not To Be*.

And, surely, a professor who takes upon himself the grave responsibility of assessing contemporary history has made himself familiar with the meaning and implications of such terms of technical jargon as escalation, first strike, second strike, whole hoggers and half-way housers!

However convincing the claim of superiority for contemporary historical writing from Thucydides onwards, in the nuclear-space age, men who have been conditioned over the years to think of the writing of history in cloistered seclusion as an occupation innocent of cataclysmic consequence, would do well to confine interpretation, deduction and assessment to the history of the pre-nuclear age that can be seen in perspective. Fortunately, for dependable and accessible knowledge of contemporary events objectively recorded, there is Keesing's Contemporary Archives.

In the second paragraph of this chapter, I refer to the rule of goodwill and truth. Indeed, because wisdom and survival command loyalty to goodwill and truth, devotion to them provides the best conditions for the conception of ideas that are both wise and practicable.

This thought gives me the strength to mark out rough signposts intended to serve the useful purpose of provoking better. By way of approach to these sign-posts, I quote a few more lines from *To Be or Not To Be*:

'Even if war between the United States and the Soviet Union could be confined with certainty to conventional weapons on the Lands of other peoples, those who enthuse about flame-throwers, napalm and the like must be insane, and madder still must they be if they think either country would yield to the other with thousands of poised nuclear weapons screeching for freedom.

'Are Statesmen so devoid of imagination because they have lost their nerve face to face with the insoluble problem of controlling the more monstrous creations of science and technology?

'Thinking must be done by you and me; for in ourselves is the only certain hope.

'It is clear the Usurpers are determined to maintain the vendetta with the Communist Countries. Embittered spirit in itself extinguishes all hope of total nuclear disarmament, and the absurdity of the West's idea of partial nuclear disarmament is undeserving of a moment of our limited time. The only other idea of escape that has occurred to the Leaders of the West is universal rearmament with conventional weapons so horrible that even in the nuclear age they would not be wholly déclassé.

'Since the vain ideas of total and partial disarmament, and the equally vain idea of re-armament with conventional weapons, are deadly delusions heading for universal destruction, the need of a real plan of escape is desperately urgent. If one be found, let us be profoundly grateful and constructively critical, however difficult implementation may seem at a first glance.

'The first thing to be done is to pose the problem. Total nuclear disarmament throughout the world is impossible. Partial nuclear disarmament is an absurdity. The nuclear weapons is on Earth for as long as Man. An irrevocable step was taken when atomic and nuclear weapons were made and exploded.'

We know how to make them. That knowledge can never be erased. We know men have exploded them over the most innocent and defenceless of our kind: babies, children, women and old men who never had the slightest influence upon affairs, national or international. Thus, men have proved that they are capable of using them upon their fellows. This further knowledge is an inseparable part of the psychology of Man for ever.

Indeed, have we partaken of the tree of the knowledge of good and evil, and without goodwill and truth—spiritual power—we are its slaves for ever.

CHAPTER IX

Mewn Undeb y mae Nerth   *Unity is Strength*

THE ROUGH SIGN-POSTS INTENDED TO PROVOKE BETTER ONES

THE elimination of nuclear war by accident may be achieved at least in one way.

The nuclear weapon to pass into the hands of an International State controlled by UNO, a State without the passions of jealousy, competition, fear and prestige that now bedevil the relations between the Nuclear Powers.

In this way, the limpet deterrent of frightfulness passes out of the possession and control of individual states, each as proud as Lucifer, and MISAPPREHENSION, the fatal source of the abiding threat of nuclear war by accident, is eliminated.

Given the will, this International State is practicable. It is not to be confused with World Government.[1] What is practicable must engage our exclusive attention. So far as Britain is directly concerned, the idea has the supreme merit of implementation being independent of unanimity among the nations: indeed, it is something that Britain can begin by herself if necessary, giving to all nations a pressing invitation to join as and when they like.

[1] The Leading Article of *The Observer* of the third of January, 1965: 'The hydrogen bomb means that the days of the completely sovereign national State are numbered or the days of the planet are: within a measurable time from now, we must have a world government capable of preventing war or we shall be destroyed by the nuclear weapons we have made.'

On Tuesday, the 5th of January, 1965, Peter Simple of the *Daily Telegraph* asked a number of derisive questions: 'Who is to create the World Authority? President Johnson? Harold Wilson? Messrs. Breshnev and Kosygin? President Nasser? Mr. Tshombe? Dr. Verwoerd? Dr. Soekarno? Mao Tse-tung? Or all together in happy concert?'

As I say, what is practicable must engage our exclusive attention.

A large area in the South Pacific seems as good a place as any. Woomera naturally draws attention to Australia. But wherever the site, every guarantee that would give the reality of peace of mind should be given. Because it is the fact of the peace of mind of all nations that peace needs, it is the reality of it that must be given, not the explosive pretence of it.

Wherever the site, the host country would have to grant rights of extra-territoriality over the whole of the leased or ceded area.

SCIENTISTS AND TECHNOLOGISTS

Nuclear physicists and technologists, space-scientists and technologists and, indeed, all such people who are engaged in work that threatens the life and health of mankind, directly or indirectly, to take up residence with their families in the new State and be given, in addition to their own nationality, the international status of the International State to which they must swear allegiance.

All Member States to contribute direct to the Treasury of the International State no more than a half of what they now spend on armaments. In this way science would have limitless resources, and scientists themselves would be given back the moral responsibilities of homo sapiens. Even so, the International Treasury to be controlled by a Board of Philosopher-Scientists, who would decide whether a proposed project or experiment were compatible with the safety of mankind and the proper working of every other science, for example, astronomy: no rainbow clouds and no needles!

Duplication of experiment, wasteful of mind, materials and time would be eliminated, and, as member States increased in number, large sums of money would become available for making the deserts of the Earth blossom as the rose and for doing fruitful work of all kinds in all countries.

Fortunately, ideas of international co-operation in science are in the air. For instance, on Monday, the 18th of January, 1965, Abdus Salam, hopped in ecstasy in a co-professor's room, chanting equations which culminate in a new formula systematising ' the relationships between the miniscule subnuclear particles which form matter '.

A few years ago, while attending an International Atomic Energy Agency Conference, this professor tried to set up an International Institute for Theoretical Physics mainly for the benefit of underdeveloped countries, and he contrived to get acceptance by the United Nations—

' The idea developed into the Institute in Trieste, opened in September 1964, where the final work on his new theory was done.'

An extract from *The Bulletin of the Atomic Scientists* gives another instance:

' The year 1965 has been proclaimed as " The year of International Co-operation ". The Bulletin of the Atomic Scientists welcomes this United Nations proclamation endorsed by President Johnson. We find support in it for our own proclaimed view that the dangers that science has created for mankind are compensated by science as a force bringing nations together in common effort for the exploration of nature and common application of knowledge for the benefit of all mankind.

' Science is the first common enterprise of mankind. It provides the first common language of mankind. Before the enigmas of nature, the white and the black, the communist and the democrat, are forced to accept the same discipline of truthfulness, respect for facts, and openmindness. Before the threats of microbes and viruses, before the problems of life and death, there is no class or race, whatever new discovery or invention is made by scientists or technologists in any country will enlighten and benefit all nations. The world of science is a world of international understanding in co-operation. It is in this sense that the Bulletin has established a permanent section on international co-operation; it is in this sense that we welcome the United Nations Year of International Co-operation.'

LAW

The first requisite of contentment in any society is the certainty of equality before the law with no room for prejudice or favouritism, whim or caprice. Not only must judges, like everybody else, be subject to the law of the Independent International State, but also they must administer the law in accordance with codified rules of evidence and procedure.

Another requisite of contentment is a feeling, shared by the majority, of the law being substantially coincident with the moral law, and the draftsmen engaged in the formulation of the law would need at their elbow the moral philosopher.

However, a system of law that would be acceptable to all members of the International State would take time to formulate: in the meantime, the little work that would fall to the lot of the judges in a non-litigeous community of law-abiding scientists preoccupied with research, could be based on the law of the host country.

I purposely avoid the terms *ius gentium* and *ius naturale* because of the confusion these terms have seemed destined to stir from the classical period of Roman Law to the first publication in Britain of the Outline of Modern Knowledge.

LANGUAGE

Direct communication of thought is essential in the new State, and yet scientists cannot be expected to learn the language of every country represented. At the most, one new language is all they could be expected to learn. Would classical Greek or Latin be acceptable? Or would the rest of the World accept as official languages English and Russian, and either German or French? Provided all the scientists and their families already knew one of these three languages, direct communication would be possible by learning one of the other two. Another possibility is a lottery to be drawn from a number of languages adjudged suitable for the nuclear-space age by an international body of philologists. Computers that translate languages might also be useful.

THE ARMY

The name: Life Guards.

The army to be trained to the highest degree of efficiency in all weapons and means of delivery, and be regarded as Earth's Nuclear Deterrent (END).

The army to be subject to a Council of Generals, composed of one General from each of the countries represented on the Security Council.

The first General Officer Commanding to be chosen by lottery from the members of the Council of Generals, the term of office to endure for one year. The second and successive appointments to be made by alphabetical order of surname.

No nuclear weapon to be used against any nation except on the instructions of the Secretary General of UNO, acting on the authority of a four-fifth majority of the General Assembly.

THE CONSTITUTION

A Constitution to be drawn by constitutional lawyers and political philosophers.

CHAPTER X

THE INTERNATIONAL STATE

As emphasized in Chapter VIII, the rough sign-posts are intended to provoke better: the aim must be to give satisfaction to countries on what may be called adjectival matters; for the reality of peace of mind is vital.

It is only on the existence of an International State in possession of the nuclear deterrent that there seems no room for argument.

The simple truth is that no nation or group of nations is morally fit to have the rest of the world in its power, and a safe means must be provided of lodging that power outside particular States. In this way, the frightened peoples of the world would have peace of mind to enjoy life, and their governments would have more money to spend on the development of their respective economies with something to spare for those of other countries.

The certain consequence of the 'International State' in control of Earth's Nuclear Deterrent (END) is the end of the long melancholy era of war between men, and the beginning on Earth of the era of peace: the inescapable alternative is a thermo-nuclear war and the end of Man.

If the phantasm, disarmament, still obscures reality, remember there is nothing in the history of disarmament conferences from the days of Arthur Henderson of Great Britain to the present day that gives the slightest hope of ultimate agreement. Disagreement on disarmament does not lie at the door of Communism as the propagandists of the West assert. They also assert that war lies at the door of Communism, conveniently forgetting the invasion of Russia in 1918, intended, among other things, to keep Russia at war against the will and ideals of the Communist regime. How they attribute war to Communism so soon after the second Berlin-made World War, I do not know, a war in which the

Soviet Union fought valiantly at a cost of 25,000,000 lives, against what the British Prime Minister of 1939 called 'the evil thing' let loose upon mankind by Capitalist Germany, a Germany exultant at the prospect of a world at her feet for a thousand years! It seems fantastic they have to be told of the wars that crowd the pages of history before Karl Marx and Lenin were born, and that it was partly because war seemed endemic in capitalist economies that Communism came into being in Russia.

But even if agreement upon disarmament were possible, what effect would officious and suspicious peripatetic inspectorates have? Imagine a McCarthy inspectorate in the Soviet Union and a Molotov one in the United States. Could a better device be invented for perpetuating the friction between the two countries?

So with the conventional weapons and the limited wars that every so often titillate Washington. Translated, this means the United States has no intention of attracting to herself nuclear missiles from the Soviet Union, if or when an outpost in Europe is attacked. An outpost in Europe could, of course, be protected by an independent NATO with strategic-nuclear missiles of its own. NATO, however, is not independent: as a matter of course, NATO's forces are commanded by a senior American officer responsible to Washington, and because Washington knows the Soviet Union would rain nuclear missiles upon the Principal if the Agent attacked the Soviet Union with strategic nuclear missiles, Washington would disallow their use by NATO. There is to be only one finger on the Western nuclear-button, and, as Walter Lippmann, Dean Acheson and the President have made abundantly clear, that finger is the finger of the President of the United States of America, a man, like everybody else, subject to the limitations imposed by environment and heredity.[1] Indeed, even if strategic nuclear missiles

---

[1] 'The individual appears so small in the universe of events; he is so straitly bound by heredity, by ignorance and by circumstance; the alternatives before him are so limited, the space for manœuvre so small.' The Historian and Character. By Professor David Knowles. Cambridge University Press.

seemed to be put at the disposal of NATO by the United States, they would have no value as a deterrent for the immediate protection of any outpost in Europe. The sole exception is the ' Hole in the Iron Curtain '—Berlin: hence the need of the strident threats to defend Berlin even with nuclear weapons.

In other words, to those who believe limited wars can remain limited, as is believed in Washington, Britain as a nuclear base is being used exclusively for the defence of the United States. The belief that Britain is herself defended is the biggest hoax in history, and the enormity of it is not lessened by the spectacle of British Statesmen having raw American wool pulled over their eyes.

If, therefore, the relations between the Soviet Union and the United States approached breaking point over Berlin, Indo-China, Cuba or some other place, the Soviet Union of a Stalin might, in desperation, yield to the temptation of resorting to extreme measures short of drawing upon herself the American nuclear deterrent. These extreme measures might be a sudden nuclear attack upon Britain, not as Britain, but as an American nuclear base for attack upon the Soviet Union. A feared show-down with the United States would create the military obligation of eliminating all American outposts before the final confrontation.

Now, resuscitation of a dead Britain is beyond the power of retaliation. Retaliation would merely mean a dead Russia and a dead America. Do British Ministers believe the United States would have to die by her own act because the whole of Britain had made the supreme sacrifice? Do Ministers seriously believe the United States would elect to die for nothing? Do Russians? I am certain the Soviet Union believes morality, on the one hand, and the care of self on the other, make nonsense of unrealistic promises to Britain that could neither benefit by, nor be interested in their implementation; for the tomb of the Unknown Soldier in Westminster Abbey would have merged into the tomb of the 53,000,000 people of Britain.

Concede the premise, self-preservation, and the conclusion

I have stated is inescapable. Professions of intentions thought of as good and genuine by the Americans who make them are a dangerous irrelevance: indeed, in practical effect upon us, the more genuine, the more lethal.

What I have said of the American deterrent and Britain applies also to the Federal Republic of Germany. Its government, therefore, would do well to accept what is a law of nature: there is nothing it can do to give 'credibility' to the American deterrent. If ever the Soviet Union were goaded into implementing the First Strike Nuclear Strategy against Europe, there would be no one in Europe in whose favour the United States could retaliate. Notwithstanding irrational promises to Europe, retaliation would be a gross betrayal of the people of the United States, and the first duty of every national government is the preservation of its own people. Is it conceivable the government of the land of the Monroe Doctrine would be less concerned with the preservation of its people than other governments?

The situation analysed, one sees Britain existing on Russian sufferance, and if the Soviet Union be the monster she is made out to be, British abuse of her is fraught with the gravest peril to Britain.

As we have no anti-missile missiles, as the Russians are feared to have, it is our bounden duty to the past, present and future of this land of Britain to consider the effect upon it of an all-out nuclear attack. Would it be war, or massacre and obliteration? In a matter so definitively fatal, it is the duty of every one of us as individual citizens to rely upon our own common sense and not upon the claims of experts expressed through the mouths of Ministers. It is our duty to recall their proud boasts in the 'thirties: the fire-power of our Capital Ships was to blast from the skies all hostile aeroplanes: in a few minutes the *Prince of Wales* and the *Repulse* were at the bottom of the sea.

The major Policy Speech in 1961, delivered by a British Prime Minister to the élite of the United States after conferences with the President, confronted Britain with major disaster. If it be as true as it appears to be that there is less of the Leader in British Leaders after every meeting with an American President, how many times can a British Leader meet an American President before disappearing from the political scene? The Leaders of British Political Parties would do well to ponder upon the basic cause of Macmillan's confusion.

Reluctantly, I am forced to the conclusion that the Capitalist Countries show no sign of yielding a statesman equal to the demands and opportunities of modern times: their mentality is the parochial mentality of an age that is passed, the mentality of balances of power and division that spell certain destruction in the nuclear-space age.

With urgency and hope I turn from the mental processes of experts geared to the past to the common sense of the ordinary people as a first practical step towards the creation of the International State.

To inaugurate the way of life of international collaboration that must synchronize with the nuclear-space age if Man is to survive, the following kind of programme could be adopted by a British National Government:

A cordial message of goodwill to all countries, including Germany and the United States, the Soviet Union and the People's Republic of China.

A personal statement to the Head of every government of the intention of Britain to take the first opportunity of submitting to the General Assembly of UNO a plan for an International State with the exclusive possession of Earth's Nuclear Deterrent (END), the statement to declare the intention of Britain to proceed with the plan all alone if necessary, with a pressing and standing invitation to every other country to join.

Britain to resign immediately from NATO; withdraw all forces from Europe; request the United States to withdraw all forces and technicians from Britain; RENOUNCE THE NATIONAL USE OF ATOMIC AND NUCLEAR WEAPONS; trade freely and fairly with all countries, treating all respectfully as fellow-members of the family of nations on our ever-contracting tiny planet, Earth.

The case against the proliferation of atomic and nuclear

70

Independent Sovereign States is indisputable, and that in itself is a compelling reason for speedy co-operation and collaboration between the United States and the Soviet Union.

Though thrust upon them by self-preservation, collaboration in practice would almost certainly engender a consciousness of common trusteeship of life, and, with fellowship taking the place of bitter rivalry and suspicion, the way would be open for the two Colossi in the faith of established friendship to share their costly burdens with the new International State suggested in these pages.

For, as the proliferation of atomic and nuclear Independent Sovereign States is unthinkable, so is unthinkable the existence of all other States being dependent upon either or both of the Collossi. What if the Kremlin had been stubborn in the Cuban crisis of October 1962, as it was urged to be by the People's Republic of China? The American nuclear weapons that almost encircled the Soviet Union gave it far more of the kind of right that dominated Washington thinking. Fortunately for the world, the Soviet Union was governed by Statesmen of moral courage anxious for peace. But it may not always be so, and Great Britain, France and the People's Republic of China ought not to be the only countries who are fearful of a world situation in which two countries have the rest of the world at their mercy.

However, it could be disastrous for these three countries and others to go it alone as individual States. Perhaps the survival of the human race depends upon the three joining together as Founder Members of the International State. The nonsensical and dangerous ostracism of the People's Republic of China must, of course, end.

Collaborating with each other for the good of all, the nations of the world will survive: divided they will perish. There is no other alternative.

The attitude of the West toward Communism is as outdated as the attitude of the Chinese toward Capitalism—

'Every Kingdom divided against itself is brought to desolation; and every city or house divided against itself shall not stand.'

71

CHAPTER XI

FRENCH AND AMERICAN PSYCHONEUROSES

In the booklet *Western Europe and The Common Market*, Walter Lippmann gives a glimpse of French policies. It would seem that if the Soviet Union considerately holds back her conventionally armed forces from crossing the Rhine until the French nuclear deterrent is sufficiently developed, the French, under cover of the overwhelming power of the American nuclear deterrent, could and would repel the Russian conventional attack by a nuclear attack of its own upon the Soviet Union.

In other words, the Soviet Union, petrified by fear of the United States, would sit inert as relatively puny France killed millions of Russians! The figure envisaged is 20,000,000!

Actually, of course, in the grotesque circumstances envisaged, the re-active state of mind of the Kremlin would co-incide exactly with the well-thought-out plan of defence already thrust upon the Russian General Staff by the ring of nuclear bases long ago erected by Washington.

In a matter of minutes, the ashes of the stiff-necked old countries of Europe would stifle all bellicosity. Alone, face to face with the precision of Russian rocketry, the U.S.A. would instantly perceive the irrelevance of totals. Along with children, even they would understand the simple equation that 100 nuclear missiles that can destroy the whole of the United States are, for all practical purposes, equal to 100,000,000 nuclear missiles that can destroy no more.[1]

[1] Upon the subject of American nuclear weapons, see *A Strategy for American Security* by a group of experts, under Professor Millmann of Columbia University. There is also the announcement, in 1964, to the UN Disarmament Conference in Geneva by the American Director of the US Arms Control and Disarmament Agency, that in 1965 the United States will have eight times as many missiles as she had in 1962.

For an estimate of the number of people who would be killed, see Herman Kahn's *Thermo-nuclear War* and F. Lapp's *Kill and Overkill*.

There is not the slightest doubt that if Japan could have exploded atomic bombs over towns in the United States, the United States would not have dropped them on towns in Japan.

The United States has acted as much on the principle of self-preservation as any country in the history of the world. What is the significance of the Monroe Doctrine? The significance of the American Civil War? The significance of the late arrival on the scene of the two World Wars? The significance of Cuba in October 1962?

It is vital for the people of Europe to know now that any nuclear attack from any quarter upon the Soviet Union would make the United States seek peace with the Soviet Union over the ashes of Europe. The only way of saving their lives, and of compelling the Usurpers to listen to reason is for every country to join together in the formation of a safe international repository of elemental power. Perhaps the International State suggested in this small book may serve as a basis of discussion.

Also—so it would appear from Walter Lippmann's booklet—on premises as brittle as those of 1870 and 1940, Gallic logic feeds Gallic pride with the conclusion that the power of initiating a world nuclear war could pass from Washington to Paris!

Walter Lippmann also believes that though France has the same moral right to her game as the United States, the United States should resourcefully hold on to ultimate decisions, a viewpoint hammered into the luckless head of Macmillan at Nassau.

Unalterably opposed to this immoral attitude of both France and the United States is the truth that neither is morally fit to wield the power. And what is true of them is true of every other nation. Indeed, no nation morally fit to possess this power would want to possess it. If, in fact, such a nation did possess it, she would strive night and day to devise a scheme that would relieve herself of it, and place it where it would be a protection for all and a menace to none.

In the nuclear-space age, it is certain we are all of one kind—mankind—or we are nothing. Politicians who are statesmen would meet as fellow-men eager to apply the principle of the individual interests of each being the common interests of all.

Among the Nuclear Powers, the Soviet Union has perceived this historic fact. Hence the rift, on the one hand, with China, embittered in the isolation stupidly contrived by the Usurpers; and, on the other hand, with the West, made implacable by the same unrelenting people.

To-day, the statesmen of peace the world needs are men of courage, courage to stand by their convictions face to face with the hostility of friends and enemies at home and abroad, courage to stand for peace against resentful enemies committed to their downfall out of fear of their passion for peace putting an end to brinkmanship.

As I see it, we have had in recent years the fantastic situation in which the Political Leaders of the West, who on Sundays worship the Prince of Peace, have been spending astronomical sums of money on armaments intended, ostensibly, to deter from war the Soviet Union, whose happiness and prosperity depend upon peace.

In spite of prayers for peace from the liberal heart of the late Pope John, there has been little response that rings true in Bonn, Paris or Washington.

With all the organs of publicity controlled by Establishments and Usurpers, how can the minds they have shuttered be enlightened? Of course, if they had cared in the least for freedom of thought they would long since have rejoiced at the trends in the Soviet Union that are making for standards of freedom and living the Tsars would have denounced as the blackest of treason.

But fear, not joy, has been the re-action of the Usurpers. Deliberately, they suppress the truth that would emancipate the minds of the American people that of set policy have been warped from infancy. A Press correspondent in America writes:

' Conditioned Reflex.

' Professor Bronfenbrenner, a psychologist, describes the curious reaction of a class of American schoolchildren on seeing photographs of highways taken in Russia. One of the children (most of them were from middle-class university and professional families) asked why there were trees along the sides of the roads, and other members of the class were asked what they thought was the reason.

' One answer was: " So that people will not be able to see what is going on beyond the road."

' Another was: " It's to make work for prisoners."

' When the Professor asked the children why they supposed there were trees along some American roads, they give such replies as: " For shade " or " To keep the dust down ".[2]

---

[2] See also the footnote on page 83 of *To Be or Not To Be*: Chapter Seven: Cultivated Hostility.

CHAPTER XII

CONCLUSION

THE UNWRITTEN FUNDAMENTAL
CONSTITUTIONAL LAWS OF THE WORLD

As Britons are bound by an unwritten constitution, so, inescapably, are the peoples of the world: a constitution based upon the commandment to love your neighbour as you love yourself as well as upon a national motto of Cambria—*Y Gwir yn erbyn y byd*: Truth against the world.

Truth and goodwill are the two fundamental laws that must bind every State in its relations with every other; for these are the laws that science itself has made ineluctable. They apply whatever the form and nature of the economic, political and governmental system. The more inflexible the adherence to a theoretic system of individualism and rationalism in a limited State, the more inflexible the determination to maintain that way of life. The more inflexible the adherence to a comprehensive intellectual system that purports to supply a definitive solution for all cultural, social, economic and political problems, the more inflexible the determination to maintain that way of life.

But as it is impossible to be bound to a way of life without being bound to life itself, life is indispensable to both systems and to governments.

Incidentally, in nuclear war, governments will not be saved by shelters, however ingeniously planned, constructed and provisioned. Whether they know it or not, there is no longer magic in Maginot. This is an important factor in the problem of survival; for the causes of war in the pre-nuclear age that were always so holy as to insist upon the immolation of the young élite, will not appear at all holy if the immola-

76

tion of the older men responsible for the cause is to be insisted upon by the nuclear weapon. A paramount psychological barrier to nuclear war by design is the known certainty that the men who press the fatal button, together with their advisers, will themselves be destroyed, along with their respective wives, children and grandchildren, and also —and this is vitally important—along with property privilege and power. Paradoxically, prolongation of property, privilege and power is dependent upon cordial collaboration with the Communist countries: a prospect that is gradually penetrating thick layers of prejudice.

In the nuclear-space age, the peoples must know as a fact that rulers who encourage, initiate or perpetuate aggression of any kind in any part of the world are the destroyers of the system they worship, are the destroyers of the civilisation thousands of years have gone into the making, are the murderers of the human race.

Yesterday: divide, devour and dream.

To-day: divide, be devoured and die.

And they do not cease to be murderers for having the power, means and will to murder on a universal scale.

To repeat another warning: the dangers of laissez-faire. Statesmen must constantly be reminded that however new and elaborate the electronic computers, the answers will be as fatally anachronistic as the facts fed into them by minds atrophied from youth by the pre-nuclear, pre-digested mental food of tradition, orthodoxy and files.

It cannot be said too often that it is the duty of governments with a history of direct or indirect domination of other nations, whether the domination be economic or political, to establish in their respective Chancellories an independent mind-guard. The mind-guard to consist of men who know how to think, who are capable of seeing in perspective every policy planned by Civil Servants and Chiefs of Staff, who are capable of reporting to Governments in words of unmistakable meaning the essence of the plans, together with their own evaluations and constructive proposals based always on goodwill and truth—the indispensable realities.

Moreover, in international affairs, adjectival, functional or procedural matters that are thought of as 'First Things' are as deceptive as conferences upon partial nuclear disarmament; for the pundits, pupils and peoples come to behave as though all is being done that can be done in an imperfect world to prevent universal disaster. For instance, speculations and recommendations upon procedural improvements in the General Assembly, the Security Council, the International Court of Justice and in the various committees of the United Nations Organization.

No functional improvement in any or in all of the organs of the United Nations could have averted the nuclear war that threatened to shatter the world in October 1962. At the eleventh hour the survival of the human race depended upon one of two Leaders yielding to the other. Fortunately, there was one big enough to do that. In another eleventh hour with a rigid Russian, Chinese, French or American Leader in confrontation, Hiroshima and Nagasaki will appear as matchlights compared to the ensuing conflagration.

Of course, constitutional machinery in international affairs is necessary, and whenever machinery is needed, the less imperfect it is the better. Without power, however, machinery is another deadly delusion.

How useful are the gleaming refrigerators, cookers, washing-machines, and radiators that crowd the 'powerless' wigwams of North America? Or how capable in itself as a vehicle of escape from an approaching tidal wave is a crowded helicopter? Without power, without spirit, it is as useful as the grave.

What kind of nation can provide the spirit? A nation not bemused by physical might: a nation that puts ultimate sovereignty in goodwill and truth. Once truth and goodwill are universally recognised and openly accepted as binding, 'the set', 'the frames of reference', 'the external and internal limitations', will make it psychologically and statistically improbable for the two Colossi in any single crisis to be led respectively by a man out of touch with men.

78

At least one of the two Leaders will know world public opinion is behind the Leader great enough to yield.

As Christ exempts no one from the positive duty of goodwill, so no recalcitrant State, however warped by greed and conceit, however mighty, arrogant and stupid, is exempt from the sanction of capital punishment imposed impersonally upon the whole Earth by science and technology.

If the defeat of Germany in the two World Wars that she and many other nations believed she was certain of winning be not a sufficient warning of the fate of the aggressor, recall the fate of the civilisations of the past. As submitted in the first volume of this trilogy, *To Be or Not To Be*, however brilliantly conceived and carried out the plan of campaign, something fatal to the whole is always overlooked. Perhaps something as microscopic as the protozoan parasite of the mosquito that disintegrated Alexander and his schemes. Perhaps something as macroscopic as the wastes of waters chilled by the iceberg that disintegrated the *Titanic*.

Interest in the two fundamental laws of the constitution of the world must immediately be aroused and quickened into demand.

Unfortunately, people always want a sign, a supernatural sign. What a pity the play of reason upon known facts is not enough.

People still look for a sign. Before lifting a finger to prevent the approaching holocaust they want to be made certain, absolutely certain, the day is coming when nuclear war will in fact occur and destroy mankind. They know it is possible. Many think it probable. Yet, all want certainty before they will act. Indeed, they must be given certainty if they are to move one inch from the paralysing routine of their lives. Hiroshima, Nagasaki, the experimental explosions and space-flights are all signs. Incredibly, they are not enough.

Other signs are the imminence of nuclear war over Cuba in October 1962 and the five-hour bombardment of North Vietnam, as a 'manœuvre of supreme cleverness' in the

79

American Presidential Party Politics of 1964, to quote a widely read Paris newspaper. Human lives bartered for American votes. Backed by Britain!

As public-men and publicists have made so mean a use of the opportunities they monopolise, I shall now examine the claim of self-defence put forward by the United States in justification of their murder and mutilation of civilians thousands upon thousands of miles away.

The public-men and publicists of the West have fallen into the trap set for them by the Usurpers of the United States. They have looked at the pin-prick naval engagement as they were intended to look at it, from the time when the three small patrol boats gallantly set course for the *Maddox*.

But the commencement of the engagement was the bombardment of islands of North Vietnam by naval vessels supplied and controlled by the United States, though based upon South Vietnam. The naval, military and air equipment in South Vietnam is supplied by the United States and all operations accord with the policy laid down by the United States.

In ethics and at law, the United States is estopped from pleading ignorance of the operations conducted by the naval vessels controlled by herself.

Are we to believe a country so obsessed with efficiency that she cannot leave to chance even the cheers of enthusiastic football crowds would not insist upon the closest liaison between the naval vessels in South Vietnam and the near-by Seventh Fleet? (If she does not, her recklessness is a grave sign in itself.)

Are we to believe the *Maddox*, a unit of the Seventh Fleet, knew nothing of the bombardment of North Vietnamese islands?

Are we to believe the *Maddox* just happened to be in the vicinity of the islands innocently going about her lawful business, blissfully unaware of the destruction upon the islands for which the United States is as directly responsible as she is for the operations on land and in the air-space of Vietnam? And did not the *Maddox* know, with the rest of the world, of the prolonged public discussion in the United States of the pros and cons of invading North Vietnam? The terrified Vietnamese of the north might well have wondered why the whole of Christendom, whose religion is classifiable as a philosophy of positive love, saw nothing wrong in a public appraisal of issues that took no account of the murder and mutilation of the people of North Vietnam.[1]

The pin-prick engagement with the *Maddox* was part of the war that, in fact, is being waged by the United States against North Vietnam, in contemptuous disregard of the will of the people, both of the South and the North.

The junks of North Vietnam, trying to tidy the havoc wrought by the American-controlled naval vessels based on South Vietnam, saw in the approach of the *Maddox* the approach of a vessel which, in their very troubled eyes, was another vessel of the ruthless enemy. Apparently, they wirelessed for help, and the three patrol boats of North Vietnam set course for the enemy.

At 10,000 yards, the *Maddox* fired three warning shots. It was the *Maddox*, therefore, that opened the firing. It would have been the easiest thing in the world for the *Maddox* of the mighty United States, with its superlatively good navy, to turn round and make off at full speed. Who would have failed to applaud her chivalry? Instead, she opened fire—

[1] For what would happen to the North Vietnamese in War, I refer you to an article by Denis Warner on what is happening in South-Vietnam. The article, 'The Small but Ugly War', appears in the first number of *Weekend Telegraph*, 25 September, 1964.

On page 11 there is a picture of Government troops who 'force one SUSPECT under water: another (suspect) waits, hands tied behind his back'.

On page 14 are two pictures: 1—'South Vietnamese soldiers hold down a SUSPECT ready to force water down his nose and throat.' 2—' he still keeps silent after three hours of water torture and beatings.'

Page 12—Aftermath of a guerilla night attack. 'A soldier cradles the wrapped and labelled remains of his baby son.'

Page 13—'A small boy burned from ankle to forehead is treated by an American doctor.'

'When an action is over, the guns have stopped firing and the weeping villagers are laying out their dead and sorting through the smouldering ruins of their homes, it is difficult as an observer not to curse this war and all that perpetuates it.'

What perpetuates it? The dignity of the United States of America. See also *The Last Confucian* by Denis Warner.

81

warning shots or not. If self-defence be seriously put forward, the *Maddox* ought to have done everything possible to avoid an engagement: in ethics and at law, violence is allowed for self-defence only as a last resort.

When two of the patrol boats were 5,000 yards distant, each fired a torpedo. So overwhelmed by the occasion were these tiny defenders of North Vietnam that both torpedoes sped harmlessly 150 yards to the starboard of the *Maddox*! In reply, the efficient *Maddox* opened out with five-inch guns.

There were two incidents separated by two days. In neither did the *Maddox* suffer a single casualty. If the ridiculous plea of self-defence be allowed in a pin-prick engagement in the middle of a hot-war,[2] the *Maddox* assuredly availed herself of it.

[2] Answering the question whether the United States had violated the Geneva Convention in making gas attacks upon North Vietnam, a British Academic tied in knots his audience with arid technicalities. According to him, the Convention did not apply because the United States had not ratified it, and also because the United States was not at war with North Vietnam.

The Convention is concerned with the prevention of wrongful acts, and the wrongfulness of acts is not dependent upon ratification by any legislature. Moral people everywhere are concerned with the spirit of the Convention, and the issue of war between countries is basically a matter of fact. Pearl Harbour torpedoed the United States into war with Japan without any declaration of war. The bombing of North Vietnam by American bombs, dropped from American planes, flown by American pilots, assigned to the task by senior American officers, instructed directly or indirectly by Washington, is an act of war upon North Vietnam by the United States, and if North Vietnam so regard it, it is beyond the power of the United States and of the British academic to deny either the fact or the law. This is indisputable and does not admit of argument.

There are people in Britain who applaud the use of gas-bombs in North Vietnam. They have been won over to the view that the bombs are the most humane form of war ever invented.

According to the first explanation given by the United States, the indiscriminate dropping of gas-bombs is a way of getting at the Viet Cong who mingle with non-combatants without massacring the latter. But since bombardment with high explosive, the barbarous napalm and ' lazy-dog ' continue unabated, where is the compassion in adding another horror?

If it be claimed that non-combatants and their homes do not suffer from high-explosive, napalm and ' lazy-dog ', it would be instructive to have a report from a Commission of Enquiry despatched to Vietnam by the UN. After all, the President and the people of the United States are entitled to know the true facts. To enable the Commission to dis-

But that was not enough to appease the wrath of the United States, with its national days of prayer for the liberation of the slaves of the Communist countries. More blood must be shed, and for five hours they bombard people unable to retaliate, and they call it defence of themselves. Must semantics also yield to American power?

Fortunately, there are Americans who are aware of the hypocrisy of it all, as the following letter by Lewis Mumford to the President shows:

' From the beginning, the presence of American forces in Vietnam, without the authority of the United Nations, was in defiance of our own solemn commitment when we helped to form that body. Our steady involvement with the military dictators who are waging civil war in South Vietnam, with our extravagant financial support and underhanded military co-operation, is as indefensible as our Government's original refusal to permit a popular election to be held in Vietnam, lest Communism should be installed by popular vote. Your attempt now to pin the whole blame on the government of North Vietnam deceives no one except those whose wishful thinking originally committed us to our high-handed intervention.'

cover the true facts, the cessation of hostilities on both sides would be necessary, and this truce could continue until publication of the Commission's report to the United Nations, unless, in the meantime, both sides agreed to negotiate in the spirit of helping each other to quit hostilities without one-sided capitulation.

The temporariness of the effects of the gas is also put forward as proof of compassion. What are the temporary effects? Severe pain in the chest, vomiting and blindness. How do we know the indirect effects of this agony is temporary in pregnant women, babies, children and people who are already unwell and unnerved? It is impossible to say. It is possible, however, to say that men in the prime of life, like the Viet Cong, will suffer less than anybody else, and that they will return to the fighting undiminished in number and more embittered in spirit.

The use of the gas-bomb analysed, it is clear the bomb is not being used as a military weapon against soldiers: it is being used to terrorize helpless non-combatants.

Incidentally, here is more proof of the determination of ruthless Usurpers to over-ride the President of the day; for the gas attacks were made without the knowledge of President Johnson. It is of grave significance that airmen are again the henchmen.

Finally, it is certain the people of Britain who defend the indefensible, would denounce it were they to see their own wives and children writhing in agony from an attack of this ' humane ' gas. As they would be justified in describing gas attacks upon their own homes as barbarous, so are the men of Vietnam justified in so describing it. So is the whole moral world justified in condemning it, and in expressing the gravest concern at the increasing inhumanity of Man in the nuclear-space age.

Another dreadful sign was given over the BBC sound programme. An American commentator was asked what action the United States would take if, in retaliation, the superior man-power of China invade South Vietnam. ' Use nooks.' And so the American commentator gives a pet name to the frightful weapon that threatens overwhelming disaster. It would seem that those who got away with Hiroshima and Nagasaki plan the use of Nuclear weapons against Vietnam.[3] In both cases, against peoples unable to retaliate in kind! Who can blame France and the People's Republic of China for looking forward feverishly to the day when they have their own nuclear weapons? Absolute power absolutely corrupts in the United States as well as in the old Prussia, the old Russia and in every other country.

Other signs, of course, are the presence of Strontium 90 in the bones of us all; the increase in number of the cases of leukaemia, ' the moulding of the Earth into a nuclear tinder-box of two compartments divided by the infallible detonator, perpetual friction ', to quote *To Be or Not To Be*.

As I argue, again and again, the barest possibility of the agony of universal destruction ought to be enough to make every man and woman in Great Britain demand a National Government and Parliament dedicated to the survival of the human race.

Why is there no demand? Apathy is the answer given by all of the many people consulted. The same moral and intellectual paralysis lamented by Churchill in *The Gathering Storm*, already quoted—

> ' Poor England! Leading her free, careless life from day to day, amid endless good-tempered Parliamentary babble, she followed, wondering, along the downward path which led to all she wanted to avoid.
> ' If only the British people could have known and realised . . . history might have taken a different turn.'

[3] On the 6th of April, 1965, it was reported in London that in a television programme in Washington, Mr. Bundy, assistant in international affairs at the White House, warned China that intervention by her in Vietnam might bring upon her nuclear war.

Laments evocative of the tragic question in Neville Shute's book, *On the Beach.* 'Who started it all?' The belated cry of the doomed remnants of humanity undergoing the ordeal of waiting for the death vigilance would have prevented.

Apathy of the people is the greatest challenge of our deadly age. It is a disease more terrible even than the recklessness which thrives upon it.

Somehow, quickly, the people must be given beforehand the knowledge that hitherto has come to them only through bitter experience. Since bitter experience in the nuclear-space age extinguishes the people and their need of knowledge, it follows, if the people are ever to know, they must in the nuclear-space age be given in the present the picture of events that are to come. Hindsight by foresight.[4]

AN EXERCISE IN PRECOGNITION

Members of a Brains Trust in London were asked to relate an unusual personal experience. The members were Harold Nicolson, Julian Huxley and Christopher Hollis.

Hollis gave this instance of pre-cognition:

'I dreamt that a friend whom I had not seen or heard from for twenty years put his hand on my shoulder in a party, saying: "Hullo, Hollis, let me introduce you to my wife." These events actually took place a few nights later.'

Hollis is a business-man of unimpeachable character. He is also an intellectual. It is certain he saw in a dream events that did occur a few days later.

Harold Nicolson confused the issue by saying: 'The funny thing about precognition is the instances given of it are so trivial.'

---

[4] Since writing this book, my attention has been drawn to the idea of 'hindsight by foresight' being presented on film by Peter Watkins, who, auspiciously, already has the brilliant 'Culloden' to his credit. The theme of the film is, Britain under nuclear bombardment.

The content of a dream in which three pencils are put together on a table so as to make a verticle equilateral triangle is not a world-shattering picture. Nevertheless, if, a few days later, the dreamer were to walk into a room and see three pencils put together as in the dream, he would naturally feel astonished.

It is the fact of seeing in a dream an event before it occurs in time, that is significant: the quality or importance of the event is an irrelevance. I expected Huxley, the scientist, instantly to perceive the fallacy of Nicolson's response, but, perhaps, Huxley, the sceptic, chose to escape in the confusion of Hollis's embarrassment.

Incidentally, if Hollis had dreamed of a sordid crime, it may be doubted whether triviality would have been imputed. What an indictment of our civilisation that a re-union of old friends on a happy social occasion is regarded as trivial by so distinguished a man!

A Journal of Precognition would record as fact clear-cut representational pictures of events which have not yet occurred in Time, and, in proof of which, until they occur, there is no evidence of the kind insisted upon in a judicial tribunal restricted to direct, circumstantial or material evidence of past events observed or observable by one or more of the five senses.

However, in precognition, the unqualified statement of occurrences that are going to happen is not a statement of probability: it is held to be as much a statement of fact as a statement of events we saw yesterday. We see an occurrence that, in Time, has not taken place; but we would not see it at all if the occurrence were not an unavoidable certainty.

In the concept, precognition, facts perceived are as authentic and unalterable a record of events as events objectively recorded in the past tense in history books by historians of repute.

Having roughly explained precognition, we illustrate with extracts from an imaginary publication, *The Martian Journal of Precognition of 1964.*

As every child knows, at the break of light of every day, the heart-beats of the living creatures on Earth have all been drawn together by what we may think of as sensitized sound magnets, and, via Truestar, they have been relayed to Mars by a series of single pulses to broadcast in music the spectacle of dawn.

But the heart-beats have stopped. The carillon is silent. The peals will no more be heard that have uplifted our hearts for centuries with the rhythmic pulse of life from the planet Earth.

Instantly, space-ships soar on reconnaissance and their reports of impenetrable cloud of intense radio-active dust around Earth confirm the end of life upon it.

As oxygen is to the life of an individual, so are truth and goodwill to international society in the nuclear-space age. Given the fair atmosphere known to have enveloped the Earth in the final phase of life upon it, and, therefore, the absence of catastrophic external forces, the conclusion is inescapable that life on Earth perished by the hands of men in authority who ignorantly treated them as irrelevant.

COMMENTS UPON THE FORESEEN REPORTS OF EXPERTS OF THE YEAR 2970

At last it is held safe for our engineers, physicists, mathematicians, chemists, biologists, statisticians, philologists, archæologists, philosophers, doctors, architects, computers and all to land on the lifeless planet Earth became in 1970.

Philologists, having deciphered the tomes of history recovered from the vaults roofed and insulated by the rubble of the demolished Bodleian, and from a single building miraculously erect, the academic Martian learns of the segmentation of the surface of the planet Earth into Independent Sovereign States, each so acquisitive that all spent a large part of their national wealth—youth, mind, sinew, time and space—not upon making their planet more and more fruitful for the benefit of all, but upon waging upon each other as horrifying and devastating a war as science and technology made possible.

On Mars, the tradition of solicitude for one's neighbour is as much a reality as regard for oneself. The happiness and confidence of its people are the source of its advanced mental and physical culture. It is hard to believe stories from the past of the hysteria excited by every step hewn to this way of life; for, to-day, everyone enjoys a freedom of spirit, mind and body never imagined by ancestors whose way of life ministered to arrogance and servility, corruption and greed, jealousy and spite, cruelty and humiliation, parricide and robbery, war and pestilence.

It is small wonder the Mars of long ago was adopted as the God of War: that Earth so adopted it, however, is the wonder of all wonders; Earth that, alone in the vast universe, persisted on this suicidal course to her doom, and in the name of freedom silenced or ignored those who warned her of the END.

Tolstoy, for instance:

> 'One generation after another strives to find the security of its existence in violence, and by violence to protect its privileges.
> 'We believe the happiness of our life is in power and domination and the abundance of worldly goods.'
> 'To establish the doubtful security of an uncertain life in an uncertain future we sacrifice a life of certainty in a present that we might really possess.'
> 'The illusion is in the conviction that our existence can be made secure by a struggle with others.'
> 'We are so accustomed to this illusory security of our existence and our property, that we do not realise what we lose by striving after it.
> 'We lose everything—we lose life itself.'

Naturally, there is no word in the Martian vocabulary to correspond to foreigner. On Earth, the word foreigner was applied to all on the surface of Earth who lived outside the particular segment of the surface of the planet to which the speaker was held to belong.

In other words, the vast majority of the people who lived on Earth were foreigners to each other, and, for no better reason, in the periods of uncertain peace they were separated in spirit by mutual suspicion and strangeness, and in the periods of recurring wars they were separated by the battlefield of human slaughter and mutilation.

Apartheid is another Earth-word that has no counterpart on Mars. All Martians, of course, are black: as black as ebony. Like a white blackbird, however, an occasional pallid is born.

His physical, intellectual and spiritual inferiority being as conspicuous as his pallidity, the black Martians of one accord humour his peculiarities and especially his love of gold. Embarrassment is neither inflicted nor endured; for everyone as spontaneously and unostentatiously as breathing, leaves within his reach so many and so much of the material things he loves that even his appetite is satiated.

On Mars, health of mind, body and soul among the black people is so near perfection, and carelessness so unusual, that anyone who leaves property in a public place and does not report the loss on the same day is held to have abandoned ownership. All that the pallid one has to do is to take the property to the nearest Registration Office for the property to become his absolutely if there be no entry of accidental loss before midnight.

Because the people on Earth worshipped the material things, our occasional pallid one on Mars worships, invidious economic and social levels arose even within the segments, and, amazingly, the idle ones who held on remorselessly for centuries to what originally was often loot or reward for participation in ruthless conspiracy, held themselves the superiors of workers, whether spiritual, intellectual or manual. Flattery and support of amoral Leaders—gangsters, determined upon domination of others by violence, often founded fortunes of 'noble' families. For instance, the redistribution of the land among his followers by a man called William the Conqueror in 1066 in the segment called England.

Thus, because cunning, flattery, hypocrisy, greed and

callous indifference to the needs of others, tenaciously cultivated over the centuries, matured rights of nobility on Earth, a desire for the reality of loving one's neighbour as one loves oneself was either dismissed as phantasy or denounced as treason.

In the segment named Britain, it is noted the Victoria Cross was awarded to soldiers commended for conspicuous bravery in battle. This honour was enjoyed only by the man who had won it. In so far as descendants were known, they were spoken of with respect as the son or grandson of a V.C. But the descendants never became a class: the individual who had deserved the honour alone in the family was the man of distinction. And he was never regarded as the inferior of the descendants of previous recipients.

But the award of a peerage was also held to be an award of honour for distinguished service. Strangely enough, however, in social practice, the first recipient of a particular peerage—the man alleged to have deserved the honour— was looked down upon as a parvenu by undistinguished descendants of other peers who themselves had done nothing to deserve their inherited titles. For instance, descendants of Plantagenet peers looked down their noses at Tudor and Stuart creations, and, emulating their superiors, the descendants of these, in turn, looked down at subsequent creations. And like show peacocks, those who could trace descent from the coarse brutes of the Norman-Plantagenet period, delighted to parade in heraldic plumes preened ecstatically for every one of the ceremonial parades of pride that would be a laughing-stock to us on Mars. (And this, of course, is true of the humbler—the LATER—creations.)

Of these ancestors, let the Saxon Chronicle speak of the period of conflict between King Stephen and Matilda, the daughter of Henry I. Incidentally, Stephen was the man who, for personal gain and power, forswore his oath to Henry. In other words, he treated his word for the valueless thing it was—

90

The Saxon Chronicle.

' By day and night they (the Barons) filled them (castles built by the hard labour of the country folk). Men and women who were suspected of hiding their wealth were carried off to the castles and tortured till they confessed where the money lay. Many thousands were starved with hunger. . . . Some were hanged up by their thumbs and burning things hung on to their feet. They put knotted strings about their heads and twisted them till they went into the brain.'

Noble ancestors or gangsters? Galahads, Al Capones or Eichmans?

However, in Britain, occasions arose when barons and the oppressed people joined together against a tyrannical king, and, on other occasions, the king and people joined together against the gangster barons. In the result, and for other reasons, too, for instance, inspired rubric obsessionalism of judges, certain rights for the people emerged in Britain long before desperation forged them in other national segments.

In the segment named Russia, relief was so long delayed that dedicated men, sickened and perhaps embittered by suffering, resolved upon the compulsory elimination of the means of oppression for so long exercised as a matter of course.

The change-over in Russia made deadly the tensions between segments; for Establishments held together by property, privilege and power were terrified of a system that might flourish without them. It was for this reason that in 1925 a Russian Leader known as Stalin spoke of the planet Earth as irrevocably split into two camps.

This idealogical confrontation in the nuclear-space age began the last chapter of the history of Man on Earth.

The destruction in nuclear war of the beauty of Earth, of all animal life, including Man and his civilisation, end the first of the two pictures the Council has been able to present.

ALTERNATIVE PICTURE TWO

I have said: 'The unqualified statement of occurrences that are going to happen is not a statement of probability: it is held to be as much a statement of fact as a statement of what we saw yesterday. We see an occurrence that in Time has not taken place; but we would not see it at all if the occurrence were not an unavoidable certainty.' How then can the Martian Journal of precognition present two pictures?

THE MARTIAN JOURNAL OF PRECOGNITION

For the first time in the long history of this Journal, we are compelled to present an alternative picture.

In what we must speak of as Picture One, we spoke of a single building miraculously erect. Odder still, though analytically three dimensional, the psychological impression is of a shadowless pool of warmth and light that are inextinguishable.

This dynamic speck of eternity in the desolation of a finite planet has been interpreted diffidently by a Council specially elected to reflect upon the phenomenon and to report upon it.

After much thought, they decided to treat the picture of desolation in isolation, and to follow it with another picture constructively created. The picture of desolation is amplified, as we have seen, by comments upon the foreseen reports of the experts who are to land on Earth in 2970.

Having no precedent to guide them, the Council can do no better than offer an interpretation of what they regard as a symbol of spiritual power.

This imperishable beacon may bespeak the ultimate triumph of goodwill and truth; but is the triumph to be of a new kind of Man to come into being beyond 2970? Or is the picture, a picture in the making, of which the final form is not discernible because the outcome of the struggle by self against neighbour in the 1960s is not irrevocably determined?

In this uncertainty they feel free to hope the seemingly overwhelming power of selfishness represented by the desolation of picture one will be overcome in the 1960s by a campaign initiated immediately by a segment of Earth dedicated to truth and goodwill.

HINDSIGHT BY FORESIGHT IN ACTION

The nation capable of dedicating herself to truth and goodwill between nations must immediately be found. Let citizens of every nation examine their own nation in the hope of finding, if not the Leader of Nations, at least enthusiastic support in their respective countries for the Leader when that Leader is found.

I speak as a Cambrian.

CAMBRIA

Gwlad y Menig Gwynion   *The Land of the White Gloves*

At a diplomatic reception in London, an officer from the Commonwealth spoke of Caernarvon as the place in Britain, during the Second World War, where he ceased to feel a stranger.

So say all who live in Cambria, whether from other parts of Britain or from overseas. There are no foreigners in Cambria.

But no-one is fonder of home than the Cambrian. All over the world are Cambrian Societies whose members ease their *hiraeth* (yearning) for home by meeting together whenever possible.

How can nationals of other countries feel at home in a country whose own nationals abroad seem so clannish?

93

Fundamental respect for human personality seems the true answer. The talent of spontaneous harmony in song enjoyed down the centuries as an integral part of Cambrian personality underwrites the probability. David Lloyd George, James Griffiths and Aneurin Bevan were not only the champions of National Insurance and National Health, they were the obvious and natural champions of the whole of Great Britain.

Whatever the cause of at-homeness in Cambria, given its existence, necessarily ' The Set ', ' The Frames of Reference ', the inherited and environmental stimuli and controls—the internal and external limitations—or, in a word, the Ethos of Cambria, qualify her as a national standard-bearer of Goodwill and Truth in the family of Nations.

The term family is not used either sentimentally or rhetorically. As we are all subject to the law of gravity, whether we like it or not, so, now that the nuclear-space age is with us, are we all subject to the fundamental laws of the Constitution of the world, as I tirelessly iterate and re-iterate.

May not the irresistible moral lead the world needs to save her from suicide be given by the land that was Christian before Augustine landed in Kent in 597? That uniquely respects the sanctity of human personality? That has truth as a national motto—*Y Gwir yn erbyn y Byd*? That was the first to conceive the idea of a Chair of International Politics —the Wilson Chair at the Constituent College of the University at Aberystwyth, endowed by the late Lord Davies of Llandinam? That, in 1922, through the late Reverend Gwilym Davies, conceived the idea of broadcasting every year a message of goodwill by its children to the children of the world? That, through the inspired labours of Mr. Gwynn Williams, has given to the world the annual International Eisteddfod of Llangollen?

Applied to International Politics, the spirit of Llangollen would make war and preparation for war unthinkable. Since 1947, citizens from as many as fifty countries have come

94

together to enjoy with each other the folk-music and dances of their home-lands.

Love of their art, which lifts them above man-made barriers, has made them appreciative of the maximum effort each has given to training and rehearsing, and the generous applause they give to the performances of others, blends with the warmhearted welcome and hospitality all receive from the people of and around Llangollen—the people of Cambria, where citizens of other countries are at home.

Those who admit as a distinct possibility the suicide of Man, but who doubt the possibility of applying to nations the principles of goodwill and truth that would certainly save him, would do well to stay in Llangollen for the whole of the Eisteddfod to see for themselves goodwill and truth in action between men and women of many lands. The unexpected warmth of the applause that greeted the performance of a fearful group from West Germany reduced the group to tears—tears of joy.

In case Cambria be the nation with the mind, will and heart needed to initiate the moral campaign that can save Earth from the calamity of a nuclear war, and from the disgrace of spending annually thousands of millions of pounds on implements of human butchery, let us waste no time in considering what action to take.

Apply immediately the principle, *mewn undeb y mae nerth*—unity is strength. Work hard in every village and town to send to the House of Commons in Westminster Members committed to goodwill and truth in home and in foreign affairs, committed also to the formation of a British National Government similarly bound.

Establish a monthly journal on International Affairs, committed, like Members of Parliament, to goodwill and truth between nations so that all nations will come to look upon them as the axis around which Life revolves in the age of the rocket, the space-craft and the nuclear weapon.

Cambrians, everywhere, to be invited to subscribe in advance for twelve issues every year so as to make the journal, from the beginning, independent of the tyrannical power of the sectional interests that advertise.

Perhaps it would be possible to work in close collaboration with the Wilson Chair of International Politics at Aberystwyth. I recall the stimulating effect of the lectures of Alfred Zimmern to crowded audiences in Aberystwyth, Cornell and Oxford, in which newspapers, journals, histories, biographies, published official papers and the like were subjected to the penetrating rays of truth. The same kind of examination could be broadcast to the world two or three times a week on a Cambrian wavelength. I believe such broadcasts would soon be eagerly awaited in the same way as Churchill's stark speeches were awaited in the early 'forties by peoples at long last alive to the power of truth.

APPENDIX

Two articles follow that are intended to demonstrate the different conclusions analyses based on goodwill and truth give from the partisan ones of special pleading:

    1. The Nascent States of Africa.
    2. Goa.

1.—THE NASCENT STATES OF AFRICA

IF in a country that has given to the world the Mother of Parliaments, Professor Max Beloff, as an academic, and Lord Boothby, as a parliamentarian, on considerable evidence conclude that power has passed from the House of Commons and the Cabinet to one man, the Prime Minister, is it reasonable or fair to expect perfection of democracy in a new State?

Consider the difficulty of a new State like the Congo— tribalism, resentments of chiefs, superstitions, the personal ambitions, jealousies and rivalries that exist there, as they exist everywhere, the vested interests of foreigners eager to play one faction against another, the almost universal illiteracy of an emotional people.

Theoreticians blind to these realities incite unrest and confusion, civil war and chaos. Terrifyingly in love with their own virtue, these people would irresponsibly turn Ghana into a Congo.

What would be the fate of the new States of East Africa in 1964 if the request for British help to put down the rebellions had been refused? Would a constitutional Opposition eager for office, fame and power have achieved stability? Would they have restored order? Order was restored by force. Is order that is established by foreign force right, and order that is established by native force wrong?

Wholehearted support to the Head of his Country is the true patriotism in an emergent State. Fortunately, the Leaders of the African State are men of considerable moral stature. Indeed, they are moral giants compared to William Rufus and his kind.

The duty of every educated and skilled African is to give without stint of ideas, expertise, knowledge and wisdom in committee or the like, and, for the present, to accept the decision of the Leader and to work for its success as single-mindedly as ambassadors work for the success of policies they have opposed in conference.

The men who best serve the new State are those who give freely in establishing and maintaining the stability from which the good things of life can grow. As they succeed, so will the equation of pallidity of skin, being equal to moral and intellectual perfection, recede into the background of discarded nonsense. As they succeed, so will the discrimination against colour in the Union of South Africa and in the United States of America be seen to be as baseless as it is base. Indeed, stabilise at home, and, at home, dissipate apartheid abroad.

In his book, *The Evolution of Modern Europe*, Sir J. A. R. Marriott says: 'A strong executive is essential to economic prosperity but never was the central government in England less efficient than under the Lancastrian kings. As in Italy during the half-century that followed the attainment of unity, so in the England of the 15th century, it was manifest that the development of the constitutional machinery has gone too fast. PARLIAMENTARY GOVERNMENT IS THE VERY WORST FORM OF GOVERNMENT UNLESS A PEOPLE ARE READY FOR IT. The English Parliament, as a great historian has observed, was not, at that time, ready "for the efficient use of the liberties it had won. . . . Constitutional development had outrun administrative order ".[1] The result was seen

[1] Stubbs, *Constitutional History.*

in the lawlessness of the baronial oligarchy, in the social anarchy of which the Wars of the Roses were the characteristic symptom.' . . . ' Whatever else may be said of the Tudors, it cannot be denied that they gave the Country strong government, the discipline and repose essential to political and social recuperation. The effect was seen in the national efflorescence, which threw lustre on the Elizabethan era.'

The patriots of nascent States are those who give to the uttermost in establishing and maintaining stability, and, in turn, national efflorescence will throw lustre upon the great era of consolidation of their respective countries.

2.—GOA

BRITISH criticism of the expulsion of the Portuguese from Goa revived in India a demand for secession from the Commonwealth.

Those who hope for the moral integration of all the countries of the world would deplore a secession that would weaken an existing group of Independent Sovereign States so bound together that war between them would shock even this war-ridden world.

Many enjoyed the luxury of hectoring the one Statesman in the world, who, by general acceptance, passionately wanted international problems solved by negotiation and, increasingly, by negotiation between minds free from duress.

It is with genuine regret that others felt compelled to criticise Mr. Nehru, while the majority, on this, as on most problems of International Politics, could do no other than allow accredited spokesmen and writers to make up their minds for them.

Probably all, except the obdurate of harsh prejudice, wish in their hearts for the triumph of goodwill and truth. Since, however, the obdurate have the intention, determination and opportunity of capturing the minds of the majority, the majority scarcely ever suspect their weight of numbers is used of set-purpose to crush the ideals cherished in their hearts.[1]

Over the years, the ideals of goodwill and truth have been interwoven with the name of Nehru, and I believe the invasion of Goa must be explicable in these terms.

The period of fourteen years that was allowed to pass between the voluntary departure of the British and the forcible departure of the Portuguese is the first fact to grasp.

Few will dissent from the proposition that the period of fourteen years over and above the many years it took Britain to have her mind definitively made up to go, was more than enough for Portugal to arrive at a similar decision. Surely, holding back his hand over these weary years in the forlorn hope of a change of heart in Portugal is consistent with Nehru's devotion to the principle of peaceful solution of international disputes.

Or does devotion to this principle require its adherents to stand by for ever and allow their fellow-Indians to be held down in subjection by the terrorists of Angola? What can the victims of terrorism in Angola think of any principle of so-called International Law that condemns them and their issue to live out their lives on Earth in subjection?

When will the Whites of 'The Free World' have the common sense and the common decency to see that the Writ of International Law made by Whites for Whites has no moral authority in communities of men held down by aliens who deny their manhood?

To those who believe in the sanctity of human personality, the conclusion is inescapable that the physical violence strictly needed to strike off fetters from human beings is morally superior to a law that, in practice, makes the fetters irremovable. That is why we British thank our ancestors for Magna Charta and The Bill of Rights. That is why unborn Asians and Africans will thank their ancestors for bequeathing freedom.

[1]See footnotes on pages 82 and 83 of *To Be or Not To Be*, which give extracts from *Man of the World* by Cornelius Vanderbilt.

Now, as year followed year, Nehru must have feared that nothing less than a miracle could bring about the voluntary withdrawal of the Portuguese. They had ruled Goa for centuries, and had come to think of it as a part of Metropolitan Portugal. With the best will in the world toward all countries, no government of the moment could feel so sure of itself as to abdicate sovereignty over Goa.

It is unrealistic to expect Salasar or any successor to be driven by some inner irresistible moral force to cut off from Portugal the thinking and policy of centuries. But even if they were so driven, would they survive the amputation?

Surely, it is fair to say there was neither the will nor the power either in Portugal itself or in UNO to give freedom to the Indians of Goa: the will and the power were to be found in India alone. Somehow, this side of the question has escaped the notice of the friendly critics of Nehru who had expected Time to dissipate the anomaly and anachronism of Goa.

Inevitably, the question is put whether it is right for India to want the inhabitants of Goa to govern themselves democratically in association with their countrymen. The answer will escape us if we fail to take account of the insufferable attitude of superiority affected by the West. Because the colour-bar has bruised the mind of Asia and Africa, the West has made it psychologically impossible for any self-respecting Indian to tolerate in the sub-continent of India any vestige of Western domination.

In extinguishing the Portuguese rule of Goa, Nehru did for Portugal what no passing ruler of Portugal could be expected to do. At the same time, the Indians have helped themselves to the full nationhood their old civilisation insistently demanded.

It is surprising the intellectual admirers of Nehru who regretted violence in Goa alleged no inconsistency in the use of Indians in the Congo. An out and out pacifist, of course, would not use force anywhere. Indeed, it may well be questioned whether he could allow in his own country even an army for defence. Obviously, Prime Minister Nehru did not profess pacificism in this sense; for he recruited, trained and equipped an army, and, at the request of UNO, he sent contingents of it overseas on active service.

No-one can imagine Nehru yielding to the request of UNO if UNO intended using Indian forces for unethical purposes. However true a moral force UNO may become, for the present, no Leader of the moral stature of Nehru could be expected to take the activities of UNO for granted. In the Congo, as in Goa, Nehru's army fought for freedom. In these two places, as in the General Assembly of UNO in September 1960, when, with four other Leaders, he fought for a reconciliation between Mr. Krushchev and President Eisenhower, the late Prime Minister Nehru took his stand for peace.

Admirers of Nehru also feared the use of violence in Goa would encourage lawlessness in the world. This is an exciting theme for academic discussion; but when we descend from the distraction of abstraction to the realities of International Politics, we find the Powers who threaten universal destruction by a thermo-nuclear war for the lie of the liberty of West Berlin, constitutionally impervious to anything said or done by Mr. Nehru or by anyone else, however good, however wise.

The liberation of the Indians of Goa will not in the slightest degree make the Nuclear Powers less or more mindful of their trusteeship of Life. Indeed, in a world of warring nations armed to the teeth, the Army of Nehru set a high moral standard in using no more force than was strictly necessary in its mission of liberation. However, as we succeed in having the fundamental constitutional laws of goodwill and truth universally applied, so will international problems be resolved without recourse to war.